DATE			
OCT 1 8 1993			

Urban Survival

Urban Survival

THE WORLD OF WORKING-CLASS WOMEN

Ruth Sidel

BEACON PRESS   Boston

Beacon Press books are published under the auspices
of the Unitarian Universalist Association
Published simultaneously in Canada by
Fitzhenry & Whiteside Ltd., Toronto
Printed in the United States of America

(hardcover) 9 8 7 6 5 4 3 2 1

Grateful acknowledgment is made to Dover Pub-
lications, Inc., for permission to reprint four lines from
a song composed by James Oppenheimer as it appears
in *Songs of Work and Freedom,* edited by Edith Fowkes
and Joe Glazer, 1960.

Library of Congress Cataloging in Publication Data
Sidel, Ruth.
   Urban survival.

   Bibliography: p.
   1. Women—United States—Social conditions—Case
studies.   2. Women—Employment—United States—
Case studies.   3. Labor and laboring classes—United
States—Case studies.   4. Women—United States—
Attitudes.   I. Title.
HQ1426.S45 1978   301.44'42'0973   78-53658
ISBN 0-8070-3796-6

Acknowledgments

I am deeply grateful to the women whose words and experiences are the heart of this book; they participated in this collective effort with warmth and generosity. I thank them for sharing their lives and for their friendship.

This book was written in partial fulfillment of requirements for a doctoral degree from Union Graduate School. The members of my doctoral committee, Rita Arditti, Frances Brisbane, Donna Katzin, Rayna Rapp, and Sumner Rosen have made important contributions, particularly in the areas of research methodology and the presentation of the material. I thank them.

I am also deeply grateful to Phoebe Weber who has from the beginning been intimately involved in the conceptualization and realization of this book. She put me in touch with several of the women, indefatigably transcribed almost all of the tapes, typed repeated drafts of the manuscript, and, most important, was always there with words of encouragement.

To Charlotte Cecil Raymond of Beacon Press and to Ruth Artig, Monnie Callan, Luna Carne-Ross, Rita Eisenberg, Miriam Hernandez, Sharon Lockett, Norma Shuldiner, and Sally Kohn, my thanks for their help with various aspects of the manuscript. And finally, the book could not have been written without the encouragement, advice, and love of my husband, Victor W. Sidel, and of our sons, Kevin and Mark Sidel.

Contents

Urban Survival

Introduction

A muffled explosion at about 4:30 in the afternoon was the first warning anyone had that March 25, 1911, would be different from any other Saturday in industrial history. Smoke billowed from the eighth floor of the Asch Building on Greene Street and Washington Place, the middle floor of the three which housed the Triangle Shirtwaist Company. One passerby saw what he took to be "a bale of dark dress goods" being thrown out of a window. Another who saw it thought the factory owner was trying to save his cloth from the fire. But then the screams began. It had not been a bundle of cloth, but a human being, leaping from the window. Then came another, and then another.[1]

The Triangle Shirtwaist Company fire of 1911 was an unforgettable tragedy in the history of the American working class and particularly in the history of American working-class women. One hundred and forty-six workers, most of them girls and women, suffocated, were burned, or jumped to their death that day. The doors to the factory had been locked to "keep the women in and the organizers out"; there was no sprinkler system; no fire drills had been held; and the doors opened inward rather than out.[2]

Nearly sixty-five years later Pauline Newman, a long-time organizer and education director of the International Ladies' Garment Workers Union, described the working conditions in the garment industry at the turn of the century that led to the "Uprising of the 20,000" (the historic strike in 1909–1910 of New York shirtwaist workers), and ultimately to the tragic fire:

I went to work for the Triangle Shirtwaist Company in 1901. The corner of a shop would resemble a kindergarten because we were young, eight, nine, ten years old. It was a world of greed; the human being didn't mean anything...

Most of the women rarely took more than $6.00 a week home, most less. The early sweatshops were usually so dark that gas jets burned day and night. There was no insulation in the winter... Of course in the summer you suffocated with practically no ventilation...

The condition was no better and no worse than the tenements where we lived...

We wore cheap clothes, lived in cheap tenements, ate cheap food. There was nothing to look forward to, nothing to expect the next day to be better.

Someone once asked me: "How did you survive?" And I told him, what alternative did we have? You stayed and you survived, that's all.[3]

As Newman stated, "... that world ... has no resemblance to the world we live in today,"[4] but working-class women in New York City are still struggling three-quarters of a century later to build satisfying lives for themselves and their families, and many are indeed still struggling to survive. The forms of the city's inhumanity have changed; child labor is no longer a fact of life, and working and living conditions have improved dramatically. But working-class women today are often faced with other forms of inhumanity: routinized, insecure jobs that pay salaries barely sufficient to feed and clothe a family; frequent periods of unemployment, particularly for members of minority groups; deteriorating neighborhoods in which physical safety is a primary concern; and inadequate, often insensitive, human-service institutions. Yet they, like the shirtwaist workers of the early 1900s, must stay and survive.

Working-class women generally do not have the opportunity to describe their lives, their daily reality, their hopes, and their fears without an intermediary, an interpreter who is invariably from a very different social class. What I have tried to do in this book is to give eight working-class women an opportunity to communicate with us directly about the problems of survival in the city today.

According to Andrew Levison, three-fifths or sixty percent of the population of the United States are members of the working class.[5] The myth of the United States as a middle-class mecca of suburban homes, station wagons, and summer vacations has been gradually exposed during the past decade.[6] If we define *working class* as that "giant mass of workers who are relatively homogeneous as to lack of developed skill, low pay, and interchangeability of person and function"[7] and add the characteristic of simplified, routinized work that does not require independent judgment, it appears that many of the workers who have been labeled "middle class" (particularly clerical workers, service workers, and sales workers) are more appropriately included in the working class. Even if we use a more traditional definition of working class (i.e., "those engaged in the production and distribution of material goods and services who do not own or control the object of their labor or its uses"[8]) we arrive at the same conclusion—that craftsmen, clerical

workers, operatives, sales workers, service workers, and nonfarm labor-
ers are, as Harry Braverman claims, "unmistakably" part of the working-class population.[9]

If, indeed, sixty percent of all Americans can be described as
"working class," then the lives and concerns of working-class women
have been singularly neglected in the recent outpouring of books on
women. There are, of course, significant exceptions to this malignant
neglect[10] but, for the most part, the lives and concerns of the middle
class, the upper-middle class, and of superstars—women who because
of birth, marriage, or achievement are deemed worthy of our special attention—have dominated the literary scene.

Moreover, while some recent writing about working-class women
has been sensitive and has attempted to portray their lives from their
perspective, many earlier works about the lives of the working class in
our society have been, I believe, deeply flawed. These "studies" which
have invariably been written by members of the upper-middle class are
frequently tainted by a pervasive class bias that masquerades as schol-
arship. Patterns that vary from middle-class norms are subtly, and often not-so-subtly, scorned. Researchers investigating marital relationships often describe working-class couples as "slow to see conflict" or as
having a "trained incapacity to share," or they depict "less educated
husbands" as having "deficient skills of communication"; other researchers more concerned with social and political issues frequently
portray members of the working class as conservative, racist "hard-
hats" who are attempting to turn back liberal reforms designed to improve the lot of the poor. These portrayals are often drawn from the
vantage point of the liberal academician or writer, safely ensconced in
a nearly all-white suburb, whose children attend excellent, often model,
schools.

Although I am surely subject to all of the class biases just described, I have attempted in this book to minimize class barriers and
my own misperceptions by using the technique of oral history. Largely
in their own words rather than through those of an intermediary we are
given a glimpse of the lives of selected working-class women—women
who have sufficient income to provide a basic level of food, clothing,
and housing for themselves and their families; women who have sufficient education to be able to cope with our complex society, but not
enough to establish themselves as part of the middle class; and women
who continue to live in urban areas largely deserted by the middle
class, often surrounded by the very poor and the very rich. I have tried
to examine with these women the texture, the fabric of their lives, how

they move from day to day, how they juggle their commitments and conflicts, and the ways in which they put together their lives: in short, their techniques for survival.

In addition to this overall view of their lives, I have been particularly concerned about their view of their role as women. What is their role in the home when they also work outside it, frequently earning a substantial percentage of the family income? How does the working-class woman feel about "women's liberation" and equality with men? Does she think that a better life for herself is tied to a better life for men, or does she see the needs of women as a separate issue? Do these working-class women identify with the women's movement or do they think that it is largely irrelevant to their problems?

Another issue of primary concern to me is their view of and experience with human services. Over the past century the human-service sector has played an increasingly important role within American society. Many of the care-giving and care-taking functions that were formerly provided by the family and the community are now provided by human-service institutions. In discussing the effects of industrial capitalism on the social fabric of American life, Braverman has stated, "... the population no longer relies upon social organization in the forms of families, friends, neighbors, community, elders, children, but with few exceptions must go to market and only to market, not only for food, clothing, and shelter but also for recreation, amusement, security, for the care of the young, the old, the sick, the handicapped." [11] If this description is indeed correct, what effect do human-service institutions have on members of the working class who, while able to provide a minimal standard of living for themselves and their families, are nevertheless unable to purchase services in the manner of the middle class and are often dependent upon public or quasi-public services?

While it becomes increasingly clear that human services have, as Ivan Illich says, "expropriated" the caring functions of the family and the community,[12] what do they give in return? Do they, as any decent family agency would be quick to claim, "support individual and family strengths" and in times of hardship aid the "deserving" near-poor in their struggle for survival, or is the working class in reality caught between having neither little enough income to receive aid nor really enough for comfort? Do many working-class families survive because of help from human-service institutions or in spite of societal neglect?

For the purpose of selecting the women to be interviewed I have defined *working class* according to the three standard criteria of occupation, education, and income, all of which must be met by their families in order for the women to be considered working class. The occupational criterion includes clerical workers, sales workers, service workers, and technicians, as well as skilled, semi-skilled, and unskilled workers. The educational criterion includes families in which the "head of household" has had two years of college or less; college graduates have potentially too high a degree of occupational mobility, even if working in "working-class" occupations, to be considered working class. Finally, the ability to provide for themselves the basic necessities of food, clothing, and shelter constitutes the lower level of the income criterion; the higher level is rather arbitrarily set at a gross income of $15,000 per year. This figure was based in part on the U.S. Department of Labor's estimated budget of over $18,000 per year for an intermediate-level standard of living for a family of four living in New York City, and also on the fact that at the intermediate-budget level living costs in New York are sixteen percent higher than the national urban average.[13] The income, occupation, and educational level of the "head of household" was used in determining the social class of all members of the family; "head of household" was defined as the adult who earns the bulk of the family's income.

Women were selected who met these criteria and who at the same time represented a diversity of age, ethnic background, and race, occupation, educational level, and marital status. All of the women live in New York City, and I was referred to each of them by mutual acquaintances.

My original plan was to tape interviews with each woman, so that she would present herself in her own words, and then to edit the tapes myself. After considerable thought and discussion with colleagues, it became clear that this form of research—"studying" lower-income people in order to produce dissertations, books, and grant money for the writer or researcher—is yet another form of exploitation. In order to attempt, in my research, to increase the control these eight women have over their own lives rather than increase their powerlessness, I decided that each woman should have ultimate control over her material and that I would send each one an edited version of her tapes for her comments, criticism, corrections, additions, and deletions. It soon became clear that this was to be a joint piece of work—their book as well as mine—and since in some sense they had become co-authors, I also decided to share with them part of my modest advance from my publisher. However, since I had finished three interviews before making this decision, no mention was made of money until the interviews with each woman were completed.

Once the women had edited their own material I was faced with the question: what is reality? Is reality what a woman says on tape during a relatively unguarded moment, or is reality what she thinks or feels when she has had time to consider her words more carefully? Both are reality, of course, but because I was searching for these eight women's views of their lives and their world—not an outsider's view—their approval of the chapters became a crucial component in the process. Nevertheless, despite my encouragement to make any changes they wished, few of the women made any changes at all. One woman was concerned that her family might read the book and react unfavorably to negative comments she had made about them. She edited her material quite considerably, but in that process did not change the essential nature of what she had said. Another made several changes in wording, some for the sake of clarity and some that kept her words more in line with her current view of herself as a feminist.

The interviews were unstructured and open-ended. While I was particularly interested in a few general topics, I was, at the same time, perfectly willing to focus on whatever material the women presented and to follow up on material that seemed most important to them. By the same token, when there was an area about which I felt the woman was reluctant to speak I probed gently or not at all; I respected the women's rights to maintain any areas of privacy they wished and, moreover, I was reluctant to probe issues that might cause them considerable pain. I tried to be sensitive to the problem of the researcher bringing up painful material and then walking out of the interviewee's home, leaving her with no one to help her deal with the material. This is an often unrecognized form of exploitation in which I did not want to engage. Nevertheless, many of the women quickly and openly discussed extremely painful topics; several of them wept during our interviews and I think not one remained unmoved by the experience. To ensure their privacy, fictitious names have been used throughout the book.

The women range in age from twenty-three to sixty-eight, and the group includes two black women, one Hispanic woman, one who immigrated fairly recently to the United States from Latin America, a second-generation woman of Italian-American descent, one of Irish-American background who immigrated to this country nearly fifty years ago, and two Jewish women. The women work in traditionally female occupations; one is a clerical worker, one a housewife, one a hospital worker; another was formerly a paraprofessional in the field of education; two women had previously worked in the human services and are currently unemployed; one is a milliner, and one a waitress. The women range in education from sixth grade to two years of college. One woman is single and has never been married; one is divorced; two are widows; and four are married and live with their husbands.

But what has characterized all of these women has been their warmth, and their willingness to participate in this project by sharing the fabric of their lives, their wishes and dreams, their fears and tragedies. It seemed quite incredible to me that every woman whom I approached immediately agreed to be part of this book, became involved in the process, and has since kept in touch with me as a friend and as an interested participant. In a very real sense, this is their book.

It may seem like a long road from the Triangle Shirtwaist Company fire to the 1970s but now, as then, working-class women are oppressed both by class and by sex, and working-class women who are members of racial minority groups are, in addition, oppressed by racism. Conditions have changed since that tragedy in 1911 but working-class women are still staying and surviving. Until we truly understand their world we cannot begin to work together with them to alter it.

CHAPTER 1

Gwen Johnson

Just like the addict. They tell him, "If you get on the methadone program, you're going to be better," but you're not. Their agenda is not that you're going to be better for yourself, but . . . you're not going to be hitting anybody in the head, robbing them, and that's why methadone was given to most of the addicts . . . It isn't to make them viable human beings; it's to protect society.

Gwen Johnson is a slim, thirty-five-year-old black woman. Her skin is dark brown beneath her modified Afro and her almond-shaped eyes are watchful. When we first met at the settlement house where she worked, she was wearing a dark skirt, a red blouse, red nail polish, and several rings on each hand. She has a calm, self-possessed manner and is extremely articulate.

Gwen lives on a quiet street in Brooklyn in a sixty-year-old brownstone with her second husband and her four children from a previous marriage. Their neighborhood, adjacent to an enormous park, varies considerably from block to block. Some blocks have extremely dilapidated houses and shops, and others are lined with renovated brownstones. Since they have moved recently from the Lower East Side of New York, their house is still partially furnished and the rooms, other than Gwen's bedroom which is sunny and includes such details as hanging plants, have a rather dark, half-empty, temporary feeling to them. From their severe façades one would never suspect that each of these brownstones has a large, rectangular garden in the back—some lavishly planted with flowers, and others, like Gwen's, planted with both vegetables and flowers. The gardens, separated by chain-link fences, provide an opportunity for neighbors to chat and to compliment one another on their latest horticultural efforts. Sitting in the shady, secluded garden, it is easy to forget that you are in the middle of a borough of New York City that has a population of over two-and-a-half million people.

Gwen's husband works in a hospital as a counselor in a drug-addiction program. Even though he does not have a college degree, he was recently selected by a nearby school of social work to participate in a special program leading toward a master's degree in social work. When we met, Gwen was working for the summer as a social worker supervising a group of young people who had gotten into trouble with the law and were temporarily assigned to the settlement house for supervision and work during the summer months. Although it was July, she was already concerned about finding another job for the fall. At the end of the summer, she was unable to find other work and she is currently unemployed.

We sat in her garden to talk.

I was born in 1942 and I was raised in East Harlem. While I was growing up there, Puerto Ricans were the new people coming in and I was curious to know why people were always harassing them. There was one group of Hasidic Jews who had a synagogue on the block, but they lived outside of the neighborhood. There were Italians and there were Irish-Americans and I was around them a lot 'cause I went to Catholic school, but I spent most of my young years in the neighborhood with Puerto Ricans. My brother was young. My other sisters and brothers—they were away. And my mother wasn't a terribly outwardly loving mother. She wasn't the type that would hug you, "love you," as they say. I think I stayed more out of the house than in the house and I learned how to speak Spanish from the Puerto Ricans in the neighborhood. It was really strange because they didn't know English and I didn't know Spanish. We just started liking each other. I went to welfare with them, did translation for them, I was doing a little miniature social work, even then.

I think out of that whole block I was the only one who went to Catholic school, and just to get to school I would have to go through a lot of trouble on 103rd Street because if you wore a uniform at that time indicating that you went to Catholic school, it was very rough.

There were a lot of gangs. The Italians would harass the Puerto Ricans all the time, you know, put the pump on them. They couldn't come through a certain block. Even blacks couldn't go past First Avenue 'cause the Italians owned First Avenue with the markets and the fruit stands and all that. As I see it now, it was just a real fight for territory. But I didn't know what it was then. You know, when you're poor you're very narrowed into your community and you don't know too much about another people's community and when you go there you feel uncomfortable. So rather than put yourself through all those changes you stay with what you know, but then when other people start coming in it starts narrowing down further, even to blocks.

West Side Story tells the whole thing. It's exactly that era; that's when I grew up. My kids were watching it on TV, in fact, two weeks ago, and they were asking me, "Mommy, is that how it was?" They really, like, kind of identified with that period. So we got into a whole conversation about people, including blacks coming out of different backgrounds and what it means when you say we didn't come out of the same background. Even though people were poor it doesn't mean they were coming out of the same background. Some blacks came from the South, some came from the West Indies, and some folks lived in the North for a long time, like my parents whose background is from the North. My mother comes from Vermont and kind of had a little pompous attitude about southerners, southern blacks . . . mostly for not being political.

A strange thing about my mother was that she was very political. I don't care if it was freezing out there, she would go to vote. And do not ask her who she was voting for because she would not tell you. She worked for Vito Marcantonio* and that was very confusing to me because he was fighting for Puerto Ricans coming over here and getting equal rights, but he was Italian. And I remember her reading about the Rosenberg trials and crying. But at the same time she was a Catholic and volunteered for Catholic Charities for a long time. It was kind of weird because it was giving us two different experiences. We were getting one from the Catholic Church and then coming home and getting a different, political kind of experience.

My mother always told us, even when we were very young, "Be black and proud and independent," and although I would get annoyed at hearing her say that all the time, from a very young age I was around bigotry but I never really felt bad about it because I was kind of proud of who I was. You know, I think she told us more because we were very dark complexioned, and

---

* Originally a protégé of Fiorello La Guardia, Marcantonio was a progressive congressman who represented a district in East Harlem during the 1930s and 1940s.

during that time the light-skinned people were favored. The black-skinned people who made it were those who were educated, those who knew different resources, those who maintained contact with whatever was going on. So there was a lot of information that she was giving us as children.

Our going to Catholic schools was partly because my mother thought it was a better education and we were poor and she knew that we weren't going to get it in a public school, even then. But also, my mother was always greatly involved in organizations and at that time the Catholic religion was accepting blacks and encouraging other poor-class people to get involved. So it was a means of getting information right from the source, of not having to go to clinics, for instance, or go to places that you didn't know anything about to ask for service.

There were eight children in my immediate family; I was the next to youngest. The reason why I say immediate is because there was a ninth child that we weren't supposed to know about and I didn't find out about until I became a teen-ager. My mother evidently had him before she married my father, but she didn't want us to know. He was stricken with polio and he had to be sent to a hospital because he became totally paralyzed. I know my mother used to take trips every Sunday, some place that she never told us about, to go see him. I found out later. She would always tell us, "You should be glad you all come from the same father," and I used to always wonder why she would keep saying that.

My father died when I was four-and-a-half years old while my mother was pregnant with my younger brother. He worked in the Fulton Fish Market. They say he just fell out of the back of the truck. He may have had a heart attack, but he drank an awful lot. I only remember him very vaguely. I remember him throwing me up in the air. I remember he used to wear a cap. He was very tall and very handsome and very dark. She had my brother at the time they buried my father. I don't remember too much after that. I mostly remember when my mother started getting sick—when I was nine or ten years old. She was in and out of the hospital with all kinds of different illnesses. She had high blood pressure. She had asthma. She had a kidney ailment that she never fixed up, which is what she died of. She didn't smoke, she didn't drink, she had none of those kinds of habits.

After my father died all of my brothers and sisters, except for my oldest sister, my younger brother, and myself, were sent away to a Catholic school on Long Island. My mother just—she just couldn't take care of them; there were too many and she was sick. They were out there and we used to go by bus to visit them periodically on a Sunday. And then my mother got very sick and they put her in the hospital again.

My older brother had come home at that time. He was working and I used to take care of my little brother. Then one day this man came to the house and knocked on the door and said he wanted to talk to me and my brother. I said, "My brother's not here, he's at work." So he said, "Well, you can't stay here anymore." I said, "What do you mean I can't stay here?" So he started saying how my mother was sick and that I was only eleven and I could not stay here minding my brother, it was unsafe. So I said, "Well, then I can go stay with my aunt." And he said, "No, you can't, 'cause your mother doesn't want you to." 'Cause my aunt, I could see later, my aunt was one of those people who would do things for you, but then she would talk about it for the rest of her life.

My mother was desperate for us to be put in a place where we would be cared for and she worked things out. First we went to the 104th Street Shelter and we stayed there for about a week. Then they told us, they said to us, "We've got a little bit of good news for you. You're not going to be here anymore, but you can't go home because your mother is still very ill and she'll still be in the hospital, so you will go to the Catholic home and you will be able to be with your brothers and sisters." "Oh, God," I said. "No, let me live my life." But I went there and stayed for three years and in later life I kind of thanked my mother that I did go there because I think I probably would have turned out much worse coming from 100th Street with no supervision. And she knew that, too.

It was like a prep school on a huge, beautiful estate. It was an institution but it wasn't a place for delinquent kids. There were kids there who didn't have any family, homeless kids, plus kids whose parents were ill or were away for some reason and could not provide for them. But they did not take children who had problems.

Before I got there my sister had told me it was more like an institution, but when I came it had gotten much more modern and the last year I was there the weird nun left. She would do weird things, like make you snitch on people and if you did then you would go upstairs to the attic where she had—we used to call it a licorice stick—a thick black, rubber thing and she would hit you. A girl had a problem with wetting the bed, she was about fourteen, and she would make her take her mattress outside while the boys would pass. You know, sadistic little things, humiliating little things like that. But when she left, I will never forget, all the girls were running along the grass in the spring, shouting that they were going to celebrate because Sister Kathleen was leaving.

They gave you a whole lot of different values that I don't think I would have gotten if I was just in the street. It gave you a chance to think. It gave you a chance to be around beautiful things. Now I know where I get this feeling for gardening. There were flowers, pansies, everything imaginable in the garden. And it had, like, rows and rows of lilac trees. As you drove up from the gate in May you could smell them.

And you learned discipline. You went to church constantly. You did your studies. I think it was basically teaching you the discipline of life. I learned how to swim there; I learned how to be self-sufficient; I learned how to clean. I mean they taught you everything as if you were back in 1910 or something like that. You didn't know what a mop was. You scrubbed the floor on your knees and you waxed it on your knees and you shined it with your feet. You put a rag on the floor and you buffed it up and down. In fact we had a dance. We would put the record on and we would go up and down the room (*laughs*) holding each other and dancing, buffing the floor.

But it was very strict. I guess you have to be when you have that many people together. Very strict. Mostly they were strict around moral things and stuff like that, but it was a good experience. My brother was resentful of my mother, even after he got older. He says that she could have done better, but I say: what could she have done? She had asthma and high blood pressure and kidney problems and there was no money. No money.

I left there when I was fourteen, and I was very glad to leave, but before I left they told me that they thought that I had the vocation to become a nun. When my brothers came to see me at graduation I said that I was going to become a nun and they said, "What's the matter, they got your head? You must be crazy." So then I told the sisters I would like to go home first and if I really wanted to become a nun then I would know.

So I went back to 100th Street. Back to where I started from. I remember my mother picked me up at the office where they drop you off and she took me to Horn and Hardart and we had coffee—she had coffee and I had milk and some cake or something. Then we got on the train and got off and walked home. It was a weird, weird experience. I said, "Man, everything has gotten so small. Everything looks so small and dirty." 'Cause out there everything is so clean you could eat off the floor. And then the thing that hit me more than anything was the junkies. I said, "What are they doing? They're all sleeping." Everybody on the block was sleeping. So she said, "Those are addicts." I said, "Addicts, what kind of addicts? What are addicts?" She told me that they were heroin addicts. I said, "Aren't they doing anything about them? Where's the police? They can't be lying there just like that." It was very strange to me that they could be out there in the open. So she started explaining to me. Then everything just looked—oh my God! So I said, "Why don't we move or something? It just looks so narrow, so dingy and dirty." And my mother always kept her place so neat; she was immaculate all the time. But I guess she was accustomed to the neighborhood and there wasn't much she could really do. So I stayed there until I was about seventeen and then I left.

I left the house under very mixed emotions. I left the house because I felt threatened. My oldest brother was staying with us and when he drank he thought he was my father and he just went through the whole role of being the man of the house. He would tell you, "Your daddy is dead now and you know I'm the boss of the house and you're to do just what I tell you to do."

Anyway, he got very drunk one day, and I got up that morning and took a bath and came out and started to put my bathrobe on and he came out of the room and tried to attack me. I don't know where I got the strength from, but—I guess he was just drunk—I must have thrown him and he hit his head against the sofa. And then I ran out of the house.

My mother wasn't home; she had gone out. I ran to my girlfriend's house and I was crying. I told her what happened. She said, "Well, you stay here until your mother comes." So I stayed there. What got me mad was that my mother said she didn't believe me. So anyway nothing happened. I said, "I'm not going to worry about it; I'm just going to leave 'cause I don't want to hurt her. I know she doesn't believe me because she doesn't want to recognize that he has problems." I knew then that she couldn't deal with it. She was dependent upon him as an extension of my father in a lot of ways, financially and everything else. So I said, "The best thing for me to do is to leave." I was seventeen. I left school at the same time and I got married.

I had my first child when I was around eighteen. She was born in September and I would be eighteen that October. And you know I was married to a person who was addicted to heroin. Well, I didn't know, I mean I knew he was, but when we got married he hadn't been for over a year. He had just come from Riker's Island.* We went together for about a year or two and he wasn't on drugs then, so I just naturally thought that that was it and that because we met each other he was going to change.

He was working as a shipping clerk and we moved to a rooming house near Central Park on the Upper West Side. I got married that July and we had the baby in September and he went to work and I stayed home. We would go out occasionally to visit my mother or go to his mother's. Then about a year later I got pregnant again. My son was born in August of the next year so they were, like, eleven months apart. Boy, I was really miserable, because I was really angry with myself. I was just nineteen and I had two children by then. I was really angry

---
* A New York City prison.

with myself because I didn't know enough about taking care of myself and he didn't care. During my second pregnancy my mother used to have to come and take my daughter out because I was so upset. I didn't want to go out; I didn't want to do anything. I didn't even want to have that baby so soon but the only thing I knew about was the diaphragm and I was afraid. I think that came from my moralistic background, a fear of putting anything in me—that it would never come out. But I was mostly angry with him because I thought that he could at least use a prophylactic or something. Then in the last months I just reconciled myself because I had to and I had the baby and we were in just one kitchenette with two babies. They were almost twins.

After a couple of years my husband's brother came home. He was also an addict and they got together and my husband started, you know, messing and dealing in drugs and that started my agonizing thing of being with a heroin addict. He would come home high and get into arguments and I saw he was high, but he said he wasn't high, he just had some smoke and some wine, something like that. So, to make a long story short, about two years later, when the kids were about five or six years old, he lost his job, of course. And I didn't have a job either. It was the first time we had to go on welfare. We had to move out because we were paying, like, thirty-five dollars a week in that place and we could not afford that—and welfare wasn't going to pay that. So they found us a place down on the Lower East Side and, boy, when I came to the building and looked at it, I started crying. I said, "Damn! Why are they showing us this place?" It was just a rat hole, unbearable. How could you send somebody to a place like that? But we had no choice; I had no job and he had no job. We had to take it.

I think I stayed there for about two years before I even knew anybody. I just took the kids out to the park and then came back and cooked. Same routine, you know, year in and year out. He got a job for a while and started doing a little bit better. But he was still messing with drugs—you know, dibbling and dabbling—but he was what you call the professional or the sophisticated junkie, I mean the one that you don't notice. My family didn't know. He was not out there nodding or dirty. He always kept himself very clean. He didn't hang around on corners. He would never do petty things like a robbery job. However he got his money was very slick—manipulation or something like that. But then as the years went on, the habit got bigger and then I started missing money out of the house and he would tell me that I was forgetful. He said I probably lost it.

I remember one time I bought some coats for the two kids. It took me six months to pay for those coats. I think they wore them one time to my brother's house at Christmas time. When I went to put them away in their closet, they weren't there. So I said, "Did you see the coats?" He said, "What coats?" I said, "The coats I just bought." "Oh, you must have put those coats some place. You must have put them in the hamper." How would I have put brand new coats in the hamper? I'm not that crazy. Then he would say, "Oh yes you are, you're crazy." Then he would tell me that I was forgetful, that I was going to have a nervous breakdown and sometimes I would really start trying to check it out and think maybe I am, maybe something is wrong with me.

And then, the money was in his name. When the welfare check came I had to wait for him and he would go spend it, so I went down to the welfare office twice to complain and they said, "Well, it's in his name and he's supposed to give you a certain amount." "You're saying he's supposed to. You don't understand; you don't live there and you don't understand that he doesn't. I want it in my name too or make it a separate check or something so I don't have to be following him." Then I got pregnant again and he went back to work. He was working a bit more steadily, but it was the same; I knew it was the same. I always had to wait for him to come home, wait for him to get money, wait for him to do everything. I just felt trapped.

And then I got involved with an organization called Negro Federation. They started talking about welfare rights and rent strikes and housing. They showed films about rat-infested apartments—what the city was not doing about it—and tried to make people aware about their social conditions. He was still doing his thing but I had found something to make myself aware and get me out of the house. The Negro Federation was coordinated with Mobilization for Youth.* My daughter had just started in a Head Start program and I thought it would be beneficial to both of us for me to become aware about child care, maybe get into a new career or go back to school. But he didn't like that. He said they were using me, that I was a fool, that they had lesbians in there and they probably just wanted to make it with me. But I said, "Whatever they're doing, they haven't approached me yet so I'm not going to worry about it." Plus I was getting a stipend of eighty dollars while I was getting training in early childhood education. It was all part of Mobilization for Youth.

And I met some really great people. They were very innovative and politically aggressive. And there were other women there who were in the same predicament that I was—who had husbands who were addicts or alcoholics or who were women alone. It was an outlet for the first time for both mothers and their children, and there was an opportunity for us to create our own nursery, which we eventually did. So I just stuck to it and then after about two or three years I was voted President. By then the training program was finished and I was given a job as an early-child-care worker at Mobilization for Youth. I was making a hundred dollars for the first time in my life so I was just happy, you know? I really got involved—in welfare issues, rent strikes, food co-ops. It got me out of the house, out of my rut. I got to meet a lot of people and the kids got happier, because they were with me most of the time and they were active, too. It was like an extended family that you would look forward to. And then I started thinking about getting a divorce even though I had had a third child during this time and was pregnant again. And I was very upset that I was pregnant 'cause I was afraid I would lose my job.

Then one night we were arguing about something and he smacked me really hard, and my eye turned red; it was blood-shot and everything. So I waited until he took his clothes off,

* Mobilization for Youth, an agency on New York's Lower East Side that opened in 1962, was later to become the model for community-action agencies organized by the Office of Economic Opportunity in the 1960s.

getting ready for bed, and after he did that I just took my coat and I ran. I ran out of the house and I went to my sister's house. But he finally found me and took me back. But that night I prayed so hard; I don't think I ever prayed so hard in the many years since I left the Catholic school. But that night I prayed that something would happen to me—that either he would drop dead or that I would drop dead or that somebody would come and get him or pick him up. I didn't see a way out. So that night at twelve o'clock the police banged on my door. They were looking for him. It was the weirdest experience I've ever had in my life. They had evidently been following him for a long time and they finally followed him to my house that night. They looked and they found an eye dropper underneath the tub, and they took him. I was very happy. I felt that I could go and do my divorce proceedings and whatever I had to do.

It was the first time I was by myself—that I was making it by myself. I had money in the bank. To me a lot of money was almost two thousand dollars. I had saved it because I didn't tell him about it, and I bought a washing machine, furniture, and clothes for the kids. Then I started going out more, you know, for the first time. And I got my divorce. I started my divorce proceedings with the legal services of Mobilization for Youth. I thought it was going to be really difficult, but it wasn't at all. I got it fairly quickly while he was in jail, and I was so relieved and so happy. I couldn't believe that I could do it. I was so afraid to do it for so many years.

I think it had a lot to do with my upbringing—that feeling of guilt about leaving the person you're married to, the kids' father, you know. I kept saying, "I can't leave because it's their father and nobody's going to want me anyway with four children." And then when I finally left, the kids, especially my oldest daughter, said, "Oh boy, now daddy can't find us." And I said, "Wow, they knew it all the time." They weren't saying anything, but the whole time I was feeling guilty they wanted to get out of it, too. They were better, much better off. Much freer. My little boy, my big boy now, he used to stutter something terrible because he was very afraid of him. So the kids were very much relieved and I was very surprised.

He was hooked from a very early age, I think, because of conditions in his home and in the neighborhood that he came from. He lived right around the corner from me, and our neighborhood used to be known as a drug paradise. In the early seventies they did all these studies about the use of drugs, but drugs weren't really anything new. You know why it's new now? Because middle-class kids are involved. But that was happening when I was a little kid, and he was right in it and he never got the chance to leave it like I did. He was in it constantly. His father was a very, very good man, but he was very sickly. He didn't drink a lot. The mother was a drinker. She stayed home—she never worked in her life—and when his father was not there she had men in the house. He didn't respect her at all. While his father was working he would take care of the house 'cause she wouldn't do it.

He was a very intelligent person. That's the one thing that kind of attracted me to him; he was just so intelligent. He was a good person, just a very weak person. If he had had another kind of upbringing, some other kind of chance—and, of course at that time there weren't many places you could go to for help if you were addicted. It was much too early. It's a documented fact that programs for drug addicts were established when middle-class children got involved in the late sixties. I mean they had programs before then, but the ones they had were experimental, like in Kentucky, and blacks were naturally mistrustful, you know, because it was experimental and you only got it when you were in jail. But when it became a middle-class white problem, then it became something to look out for, something to get statistics on, something to set up programs for 'cause you weren't going to send them to jail. You're not going to put their kids in jail. So they got lawyers to protect them from the consequences.

Same thing with the war in Vietnam. We were talking about that last night. That's when the guys could go and get deferrals. When did that happen? When they were starting to take middle-class kids who wanted to go to college and who didn't want to go to war. Then they started showing them ways to and get deferrals. But young blacks who had to go and

drafted didn't know anything about deferrals so they just naturally got caught up in the war. But it's not just a racial problem. It also happens when you have different classes. Because when you become upper-middle-class black, you still see it within your own even. There is a difference between the upper-middle-class black and the lower-middle-class black and they let you know that they've made it. Sometimes more so than the whites. But they forget that they were there last year. They don't want to remember.

By the age of twenty-six Gwen had four children, was divorced, and for the first time in her life had a job that she enjoyed. Around that time she started seeing another man. They lived together for about two years and were married in 1970. According to Gwen, "For five years we were blissful," but now she's extremely concerned about her marriage. She says that her husband is restless, and that he wants the freedom to come and go as he chooses, which she claims he has anyway. She wonders if it's because he's nearly forty and hasn't yet achieved what he wants to achieve.

Gwen is very worried about their financial situation if they should separate. Her newly purchased brownstone is, according to her, a "big liability as well as an asset." She is afraid that they will not be able to keep up the mortgage payments and that she will lose not only her marriage, but the house as well. Furthermore, until her job this summer Gwen had been without a job for a year and she thinks that because she has been unemployed she did not have the leverage in her marriage that she would have had if she had been helping to pay the bills. She feels her husband resents the fact that she's not bringing in a paycheck. As she put it: "There are things that go on in your life that if you're financially secure you can in some way make it. You can move, you can be portable, you can do a lot of things. When you're not, it makes it that much harder."

Gwen thinks that the children have been badly affected by her marital problems. Her elder son, a fifteen-year-old boy, has been "acting up all year—he has not been going to school." Her oldest child, a daughter, is going into the twelfth grade and is doing "all right" but her next-to-youngest child, the twelve-year-old, is in the eighth grade and according to Gwen, "She just made it because I was watching her and teaching her." She tried to get into summer school but the only summer school available was for students who were going to graduate the fol-

lowing year and had to make up specific courses. There weren't even any summer jobs.

Gwen described what happened when her two oldest children went to look for summer jobs: "They went to get their working papers and had their physicals and everything. They went down there and stayed from seven o'clock to four o'clock in the afternoon, and they got pushed and crushed by all the kids waiting for jobs. One girl got knocked down on the floor and they practically stamped her to death. Then they came home that afternoon at four o'clock and still hadn't received a job. My daughter said there were girls there the night before with blankets, waiting. It's horrible the way they make those kids push and hassle each other for jobs." And so Gwen's children join the huge number of black teen-agers—over forty percent—who are unemployed.

But it's not only the kids who have to hassle each other for jobs. Gwen has been a victim of the cyclical availability of jobs for community workers. During the 1960s when money was available through the Office of Economic Opportunity for training programs and jobs, she was trained and employed, and she got a taste of what it was like to be independent. During the 1970s Gwen has been one of the many victims of massive cutbacks in federal funds for community-based projects. As she described the cycle, "They build your hopes up to let you down. I don't want to go through this again. I've been trapped in every situation." She thinks this has occurred because she has never passed the high school equivalency test and thus cannot go on to work toward her B.A. or an associate degree. Her husband claims that she could have finished her education long ago, but she responds with considerable anger: "I've been working ever since I've known him. I've only been out of a job twice in the last nine years and I've got four children to take care of. But he tells me that's an excuse. An excuse! What the hell am I going to do with them? I've just got to get myself together and take care of me."

But exactly how to do that is the question. Gwen thinks she must acquire more credentials so that she will not be the "last hired and the first fired" when funds are low, but she cannot afford to go to school full time since she must get a job to help support her children and herself—particularly if her marriage dissolves. So once again she is trapped: She cannot get work because she does not have the credentials, but cannot go out and get them because she must care for her children as well as work to support herself. Her frustration and fury seem just below the surface, just contained.

And yet, when she speaks of the women's movement, her views are not simply an expression of her own feelings but a far broader view of the directions this movement must take. She points out that the women's movement is based in the middle class and is not responsive to poor or working-class women—that it is fine to fight for equal pay but that that struggle presupposes that one has a job. What about women like herself, she asks, who cannot find work that would be meaningful and provide a good income?

I think now is the time for a lot of black women to not only be telling the story about what they went through, but to give something to the men too, because it's taking something away from our struggle when we're totally into the women's thing. I think we must raise our consciousness as women, as black women, but we must also raise the consciousness of men because we have to live in a world with men whether we like it or not. I have sons, you understand, so it's a contradiction if my son says, "Yeah, mommy, women have their thing, but why are they putting us down?" I mean boys are asking those questions now, you know. Boys we are raising are asking those questions. They're saying, "You don't like us, you don't want us. What are you trying to do? What are you trying to change?"

The women's movement kind of worries me right now. I don't know where they're at. I don't know what the hell they're talking about. They say they are trying to get power from the men, but where does that leave the poor people who can't get that power, who don't have an education? That's why a lot of poor people don't get involved in women's groups. They don't understand a lot of times the causes that the women are fighting for. They don't relate to them as poor women. They can't go to a convention in Indianapolis or Albany. They can't do that. Women should have the same amount of pay, sure, but some of those women won't be able to have any kind of pay because they won't be able to get any kind of jobs because they're not qualified for them.

And, who's going to take care of the kids? They're women just like me. I'm not qualified to take any kind of job that I would like to do—that would be meaningful to me—and make good money at it. I'm not. Except certain jobs in the community, like I'm doing now. But that is not something that I want to depend on all my life. So the women's movement is not really relevant to me.

Where should the women's movement begin? I don't know. No, I do know. I think they have to re-evaluate an agenda for why they're together besides wanting a larger or equal pay scale with the man, besides having equal opportunities. They have to re-evaluate the experiences of women for whom those goals are not relevant.

But it's not going to happen, because everybody's trying to protect what they got. Why not educate women to educate women who are like them? I mean, make somebody who's poor, like on my level, able to educate other women who probably haven't finished eighth grade or something like that, to tell them that they can be part of this women's movement, too. But there is no way, because they are trying to protect what they got. They can't go but so far down. They can go to some of the lower-middle-class people who are trying to strive, you understand, but they can't go to somebody who is making, like, four or five thousand dollars a year. I mean, they will be able to help them with social services, but why don't you try to help that person help themselves? And then we wouldn't have this chaos on welfare.

I don't think people really want to cheat the welfare, but what alternatives are there for these people? When they come off welfare, are they going to get a job someplace? In a factory, maybe, making below-scale wages? That is illegal but they don't care that it's illegal, 'cause they need a job and they're not going to tell on this man because then they won't have any job. There's a whole lot of ins and outs because of the way the society is set up. They set you up to make you be untruthful, to make you dishonest.

I never forgot what I heard a social worker say one time at a welfare meeting. She said, "When I first came to welfare as a worker, I was wide-eyed and bushy-tailed and excited and ready to help the world get off their ass. And then when I got here I found that I had to become a liar to get a lady a pair of shoes." Instead of saying that the lady needed a pair of damn shoes for her feet because she had no soles on her shoes, she had to say the lady needed an ironing board. And why do people have to pay for food stamps? Why can't they get soap or toilet paper with food stamps? That is not a luxury. And then they say—if you don't get them—they say you're filthy.

Just like the addict. They tell him, "If you get on the methadone program, you're going to be better," but you're not. Their agenda is not that you're going to be better for yourself, but you're going to be better because you're not going to be hitting anybody in the head, robbing them, and that's why methadone was given to most of the addicts—to protect society. It isn't to make them viable human beings; it's to protect society. And then when these people get on methadone, it's like a revolving door; they get hooked on methadone. Even if they are not hooked on methadone, they're not going to get a job because, wherever they go, when they find out about their addiction, they're not going to trust them. But that's another revolving door. It just goes around and around. Where do we go? I don't know, I don't know. I don't know if people really care about reevaluating where they're at. The women's groups—even the black feminist groups—they're out of touch, too.

CHAPTER 2

Christina Ramos

The city doesn't supply anything. It doesn't supply you with a fruit, with a banana, it doesn't even supply you with a mango.

Christina Ramos is a small, thin, wiry, thirty-four-year-old Hispanic woman with long, dark hair and a mobile, angular face. When I first met her, she was dressed in worn jeans, a dark jersey, and soft Chinese shoes.

She and her twelve-year-old daughter live in a three-room apartment on the thirteenth floor of a red brick apartment building owned and operated by the City of New York. In addition to the rather worn couch and chairs and large round coffee table on which books and magazines are scattered, the living room furnishings include a large television set, a phonograph, a desk with a typewriter on it, and a bookcase filled with an encyclopedia and books on psychology and sociology. Propped up in one corner of the room is a vivid, black and white, poster-sized picture of her daughter who has an animated, glowing smile on her face.

It is summer when Christina and I talk, and her windows are open wide giving her apartment a spacious, airy quality. She has a view of nearby roof-tops and at one point she leans out and says that you can see all the important institutions of the community from her window. She points out the police station, the fire station, the library, the local school, and the empty lot where a new school was supposed to be built. The lot is littered with broken glass, and she says there is a complete foundation underneath that was built for the new school. The decision to build the school has since been rescinded. The area is both residential and commercial. Across the street is a large, well-kept city housing project, Spanish grocery stores and other small shops; several large, imposing churches stand on both sides of the street.

Christina was most recently employed as a school aide, but since funding for the Teacher Corps* program under which she worked was not renewed, she is currently looking for work and receiving unemployment compensation. She has just completed two years of college by at-

---

* Teacher Corps is a federally funded educational training program which emphasizes collaboration among local school personnel, parents, and the community.

tending a bilingual community college part-time while she worked, and is planning to continue to work toward her B.A. The structure of the educational system and the processes by which people learn are of central importance to her. She discusses these at some length, using her own experiences as a student, as an active participant in educational issues in her community, as a teacher's aide, and as a mother, to explore the problems of education in our society.

Christina talks quietly and easily, gesturing frequently with her hands and often breaking into a sudden, wide smile that expresses her amusement at some recollected event. She began by talking about the first time she came from Puerto Rico to live in New York.

I was five, six—something like that—when I came here. I went to first grade somewhere on the Lower East Side. That was when the United States had forty-eight states. I always remember that, because at that time you had to pray and you had to pledge allegiance and if you could get that straight, you're not going to have time to get anything else done.

When I was in Puerto Rico as a little girl, I didn't think that that could happen to me. I didn't perceive that I would be going to a strange country. I thought I would be a teacher or I would be a doctor, but mostly I wanted a home. I would work and study and do things, but I would have a home. Home would be my base and then I would do all of these additional things, you know, and I thought I would have twelve children. But my life changed so much that I didn't want to have any children; then I thought the struggle would be just to live and live and live and live—just make it from day to day.

It was around 1948 and it was when flags were being raised. They were going to vote for independence in Puerto Rico and first you'd see one flag and then the other and my father would raise a flag, too. And then something happened and I was sent over here. I don't know for what reason. My mother, my father, my sisters, and my brothers stayed there, but they sent me over here. I went to school one year, but I didn't behave very well; I had my own pride, you know—like I knew I came from Puerto Rico and I knew I had my mother and my father and I knew I had my brothers and I knew that my flag was the Puerto Rican flag with one star, and so I rebelled. My aunt told me that if I continued to behave that way I would be sent back, and when she told me that I knew I was on the right track because I wanted to go back. So she sent me back.

The pitiful thing about going back to Puerto Rico after being here is that it's not the same feeling as before. You don't have the same illusions. That time away—whether it was one week or a year—really makes a difference because you wonder, why is this happening to me? My aunt wasn't so bad, but there was too much at that time, too many changes—school was one thing and the house was another. Then you feel these people are crazy—either they're crazy or I'm crazy. Somebody or something is wrong somewhere and you don't know what it is. I was a kid in a grown-up world. My father was for the Puerto Ricans, right? Then my aunt, she's completely different; she was married to a Mexican and she loved Mexican food and everything Spanish. And the school was the forty-eight stars and reading the Bible, right?

Then in the early fifties my father was very involved politically and my mother and my father split up and we were back here again. It was myself, my brothers, my sisters, and my mother—and my mother struggled. My mother—my mother always complained; she always worried. Her job was to worry. She was just trying to make it from day to day with five children. And she didn't have much schooling. She was always trying to find jobs—she took care of the building. It had a coal furnace—they didn't use oil at the time. I shoveled a lot of it, too. My father wasn't around at that time and didn't help much. He was still in Puerto Rico. He stayed there until I was sixteen and then he came here. You know, he was raised here, then he went to Puerto Rico. My mother's strictly from Puerto Rico.

When I came here the second time, my brother and I got put in the same school and we had to fight to be able to get to school. We got here on a Sunday; Monday we had to fight. Because on 21st Street, between 8th and 9th for some reason, we didn't know they had different groups, and some of the kids only go up so far in the block and no further—even though they didn't have a line, but they have their own barriers, right?—and the other kids do not go down to that part of the block.

But we didn't know this, so the day after we got there we were walking to school; we lived in the same block as the school. I was ten years old and my brother, he was twelve. So we're walking to the school and the kids came and said something in English, right? We tried to pass but they would block us. Then we were determined that we were going to go into the school. So they made, like, a gesture to go around, like they pointed out with the finger, you go around. So, we said, with our heads, no. We got into pushing. We're trying to go in and they're trying not to let us go in, so my brother and this fellow got into a tangle and, because they were more than we were, I was determined that I was going to stick to my brother and we were going to go into the school. What stopped it was that one of the guys fell down and my brother kicked him in the shin, and when he kicked him they all ran. So we went to school. After that they didn't bother us so much.

We didn't live there long, but I got left back because they said I was underdeveloped. For some reason I was too little—in size, or I wasn't mature enough or whatever—to go into junior high school. My brother got passed and I stayed.

Then the first day that I went to junior high school, I had to fight. Well, we got on the bus, a regular city bus. I had never traveled here on the bus by myself—it was so crowded, and I was still little—but all the kids go on that bus, you know, so when the bus stopped suddenly I wasn't holding on tight and I ended up on somebody's foot. I said sorry, in my own way, but that wasn't good enough. So they started joking and they were laughing at me. The girls were big, you know. The kids develop so much faster here. So I told them if they wanted to fight after we get off the bus, we'll fight, okay? That stopped it, but I was scared.

I hoped that they would forget about it, but when we got to the stop, they were waiting for me to get off. Some of them went out. I let them all get off. I would not get down till they all got down, and I was thinking: what am I going to do? So when they got down and were waiting for me down on the sidewalk, I got up on the stair, and when I was on the stair, the bottom stair, I was a little taller than the girl, right? This was my chance so I jumped on her and I pushed her because I had the feeling that she would have beaten me. When I did that she grabbed me to hit me but then all the girls that didn't get along too well with her said, "You don't touch her because we saw what happened and she's not scared of you." But I was scared, I was scared.

Let's say I don't look for fights but I was brought up with the belief—even when I was young with my brother, even though he was a boy and I was a girl, whenever he did something to me that it wasn't fair, even if I got the worst, I would fight him. My father used to say that if you feel you're right, you should stand up to it. Even though he never liked physical fighting. He wasn't a physical man. He meant defend yourself with words, but we took it further because if we didn't and somebody comes and hits you, you're not going to defend yourself in words. If I could avoid a fight, I would avoid a fight, but if somebody puts you against the wall physically or mentally you have to defend yourself, because if you don't then I think you're finished. The person will continue to take advantage of you. So many occasions you have to play the role. The difference is whether you are a passerby or whether that's going to be your home. And if that's going to be your life, then you have to do it.

So I went to the junior high school and I went to high school, and when I was about sixteen and living with my father for a little while, I quit school. Then my father decided that if I was going to quit school he was not going to be my father, so he left. To him education meant a lot. I think my father taught all of us how to write and read before we went to school; he even taught my mother how to read.

I decided I wanted to quit school because I wasn't accomplishing anything there, and I said, "I want to work and study." My father says, "No. I know a lot of people say that, but I know you are only saying that so I will sign the papers, but I know you're not going to do it." But in high school I didn't see anything happening. I wasn't communicating. You know, I wasn't very good in English and I moved to Brooklyn at that time and they gave me some essay to do on Shakespeare. I didn't even know how to read that well and they told me to read Shakespeare. I wanted to see things being built, things being done, things that you could see, that you could touch, and they gave me Shakespeare. At that time my cousin had graduated from school and I used to go to school with her but she was going off to work and I was there in school, not doing anything. I didn't have any people I could talk to, because when you get too high in school, oh boy, you're in a vacuum. Elementary school is closer; the programs are more grouplike. In junior high school there's still a little excitement going on. But when you get to high school everybody splits off into so many areas. It was like all I had in my life was strangers. So I quit.

Then I went to work in a factory somewhere in Long Island as an inspector of ball-point pens. That was 1959; I was sixteen and I was making forty dollars a week. But God, I had to wake up at five o'clock in the morning, take two trains and then walk to be there by seven o'clock, but I didn't work there long because I was offered six dollars more to start at nine o'clock at a place here in mid-Manhattan that made contact lenses.

For the next twelve years Christina worked for a shop that produced contact lenses. She was originally hired to do a specific job but eventually worked her way into the position of supervising the entire process. She left the company when it moved to Beverly Hills, California.

She explained how and why she went back to school and tried to analyze (through her own educational experiences, her daughter's feelings about school, and her own active participation in the neighborhood school) some of the reasons the educational system fails to teach so-called disadvantaged children even the most elementary skills. She stressed that children need to participate actively in order to learn— they need to *do*, not to simply be acted upon, and need feedback, not just an "X or a check." Describing her own frustration in school, she said she "needed to chat, to talk to people, to move around, and to do."

Christina then explained why she decided to go to Hostos Community College, a bilingual college that was established in the South Bronx in 1969 to serve that community's educational needs. Hostos, named after Eugenio Maria de Hostos, a nineteenth-century Puerto

Rican revolutionary and educator, specializes in individualized education aimed at the needs of the students. It offers associate degrees both in health sciences and in arts and sciences.

When I took the high school equivalency, I was very nervous. I didn't think that I would pass, but I did. And when they sent me the transcript I read it all and on the back in the last paragraph it said that we could attend one of the City University of New York schools. I got very excited and kept that in the back of my mind.

Then I was very active in the community, and when I was at public meetings I met a lot of people and I used to try to communicate with them. I even tried running for the local school board but I backed out because I didn't have confidence. I didn't feel that I was fit to be on the school board because I really think that people who are should know what they're doing. For me to sit there and to fake it and to plan for children—I don't think I'm qualified. I could have said to myself, go ahead, you'll learn, you'll learn, but because I really took it seriously I said to myself: "No, they cheated me."

They cheated me in the sense that there were a lot of things I didn't know. Nobody sat down with me and tried to communicate and answer a lot of questions that you want to know about. I didn't participate in any community things as a child. I was always in the park. I knew a lot in my own way, but that was because I was taught before I came to New York City. When I was with my mother and my father before everything happened, there were adults that taught me. Not only my father but other people, friends of my father. I wasn't afraid of them. But over here that didn't happen; the people that I was around could tell me about a lot of things, like getting a job, but they couldn't tell me how to read, because I knew how to read more than they did. So being that I thought that it was a serious thing to take money and try to plan, I didn't think I knew enough to be on the school board. And then I realized how I got a negative feeling about schooling, because as a child I didn't have negative feelings. I don't have negative feelings now; I love school. When I worked in the contact-lens job and had to train people myself I realized that it takes a little patience. You have to be there with the person and cater to the person. I also realized that part of the problem is that school—or maybe it's the subjects—is so unrelated to whatever kids are doing.

I was active in the schools for a long time, but it takes money and it takes time and it really gets heavy because you have to compete with people that have been on the school board for a long time, know about all the agencies and have a lot of what you call connections. And I don't have anything other than my brains. I have to be like a cobweb going from here to there making my own connections.

At the beginning they let me, they needed me, cause they probably figured this is an ignorant person that doesn't know her right from her left. So I enjoyed it and I met other people, but then it got so that even though I spoke English everybody would interpret. When I said something, somebody would say, in their own words, no she meant this and this and that even though I was speaking English. And I don't like that, you know. I want to say what I want to say. I don't need an interpreter between English and English. So I said the only way I'm going to do it is try to go to college.

I had studied before that. When IBM came out I took a course, but then after I passed it and they gave me an address for an interview for a job, I realized I'm just going to be pushing buttons. That's all you do, push buttons. It's a big thing at the beginning because you don't know it, but the reality is you're going to have a little machine, a typewriter or whatever, and all you're going to be doing is reading from a thing and pushing a button.

It all goes back to my father. I remember my father used to say when we were kids—he used to say a person could learn whatever they want to learn. All they have to do is put their mind to it and practice and practice and practice. So I used to go and get books and read out loud and read and read and read. My mother used to say, "You're going crazy, that's what you're doing." But I said, "I'm not going to let them laugh at me. I'm going to learn it."

Not to know anything is pitiful. At least you should know how to take a hammer and a nail and put it right. And I know that 'cause I learned it from other people—not in school. I had better teachers outside of school—friends of mine—than I had in school. Because there when I made a mistake they would tell me that's wrong and I said it's right and we argued until I found out whether I was right or whether I was wrong, and then we continued to do whatever we were doing. You don't have that in school. They check you with an X or a check, either good or bad, and that's it; the kids don't have a chance to go back and ask questions. It is embarrassing, you know, to admit that you don't know unless you have the type of relationship where there is trust, unless the person knows that he could go back and say, "What did I do wrong?" But when you get to be twelve and thirteen—that's the age you don't want to say that you don't know; you know everything. Whether the kid was right or wrong is not the issue; it's to be able to help them to think and do for themselves.

I don't know why I didn't learn in school; I wanted to learn. In school you have to go there and sit down, and I'm not a person to be sitting down for all those tremendous hours. I needed to chat, to talk to people, to move around, and to do. In fact, in high school they moved me back and forth so many times from one class to the other that I didn't know what was going on. The only time that I felt comfortable is when they put me in the nurse's office and I learned about filing. There I was given something complete to do that was, let's say, my baby or my task. You could master it and feel good about it.

Why did I go to Hostos? Because that's the only college that I really felt would accept me. Because it was bilingual and because there were supposed to be some of my roots there. Let's say Hostos Community College is supposed to be named after a Puerto Rican, but it wasn't only the Puerto Rican bit; I felt I could communicate with them because what I can't get through in English I will get through in Spanish. And a person that has been out of school for such a long time needs to change gradually, to be able to really say: well, I'm going to sit down and have that study habit. 'Cause to study you have to sit there and do many things I didn't know. Like I didn't know that the book had a glossary in the back and I didn't know a lot of skills that you need to really study. And I had to learn what is expected when you write a paper, that you have to type it. And you have to deal with the fact that you could take it or leave it. You don't have the father that's going to spank you anymore. You're on your own. And that's scary, too.

And then some of the teachers were tremendous women. Usually you don't see women that know all that much. Usually they know about housekeeping and they know about how to take care of a child, but to go there and see these young women and the way they treated you. I was always called by my first name, and the teacher would say, "How are you today, and how do you feel?" It's not that they say Mrs. so and so and the person looks at you over the eyeglasses and writes something down and then you go over there. And then there were men, too. You don't usually see Latin men around here who have a degree. At Hostos you can see men and women that come from the same background that you do, and they're there teaching and they have made a different life.

I have an A.A. degree—probably. Probably, I'm saying because they haven't sent it to me yet. I'll believe it when I see it. Now I'm going to go to City College. I will probably go into education, maybe early-childhood education, but I will, how do they say, hope for the best and prepare for the worst.

But you see, I am a person with so many interests and to me life is so dynamic that I don't want to be stuck in something that I don't like. I could always hope that there is a position where you could get something for yourself and enjoy it and at the same time do something for someone else. For example, unfortunately a lot of Latin people don't know how to read a lease. To read a lease you have to be, like, a lawyer. That's one thing I thank my mother for—she didn't know how to read those leases and I was the only one that was around the house and she would give me the paper and tell me to tell her what it was. There's a lot of words there, but the mechanics of it is that they're going to try to give you the least for the most and your job is to try to get the most for the least. And that's the whole struggle. I used to read it and read it and read it. And even then someone told me that I should be a lawyer. But I don't have to be a lawyer, you know, all the way up there. But there must be other jobs in fields like that.

I went to Hostos at night 'cause I was working during the day. I studied liberal arts courses; I took mostly English, Sociology, Psychology, you know, all the behavioral sciences. I loved it. I learned a lot. I asked myself so many times, what's happening to the city? It can't be only me, you know, because I struggle like hell to work to do something. So then I studied Sociology and I learned how organizations were formed in society and why they come apart. And then to the culture and subcultures and back to finding out who I am and where I come from. All my life all I did was work and work and work and enjoyed myself, but I never thought of tracing me: Who am I? Where am I? You know, like sometimes they ask you, "Are you American?" If I say, "Yes," they tell me, "No, you're not, because you were born in Puerto Rico." And if I say, "No," they will tell me, "Yes, because you are an American citizen." Those are the terms that I didn't choose, but that's what they use.

Christina analyzed the social, economic, and cultural gulf between the teachers and the students, explaining how this gulf interferes with the educational process. She then described, from her own experience, some of the impediments to true community involvement in the educational system: the lack of fundamental commitment to cultural pluralism, the way capabilities of community representatives are subtly disparaged, and the fundamental allegiance of teachers and others within the school system to the institution itself rather than to the community.

While I was at Hostos I got in to the Teacher Corps as a teacher aide. Teacher Corps is a national organization that hires interns—people from the community to work in the schools, to help in the schools, to help the teacher or whatever. They hope to recruit new, young people to become teachers. Being a teacher's aide was a fascinating job. I worked with children, with parents, with teachers, and with the principal. I went to conventions, went to meetings, and even painted the school. I learned a lot there, too. Teacher Corps had a multicultural component which I worked closely with. I liked it because it helped me to see more of what people are all about, and it's not often you have that chance. The cultural groups in the school are about fifty-fifty Spanish and black, but the teachers themselves are white. Socially, economically, and culturally they come from a very different background from the kids. It's like two different worlds. Something like ninety to ninety-five percent of the teachers are middle class or higher middle class.

Maybe I'm more soft-hearted than most because I did come from the same background as the children, but when they run out of the class and ask me a question I cannot tell them, "I can't speak to you." Since I'm from the community and know all the children, I cannot tell them, "I cannot answer your questions. You go back to your classroom and that's it." 'Cause they come to you for a reason, whatever reason it is, it's for a reason. I had a lot of free time, and the kids always want to know what I'm doing and I want to know why they don't want to read. Obviously some of the children do know how to read; they would sit down with me and read. But with the teacher, they don't even want to be in the classroom. I'm not saying that that's because of the social, cultural, or economical differences, but it could be.

Some of the children are too fast, they learn too fast, they pick up too fast even though they might not show it on records. Everything has to be fast because that's the age. That's the age of movement. Physical movement. And it's hard for them to sit there in a classroom of forty, not getting much attention, because children like attention. I don't think many of those teachers have many children of their own. They don't come from big families. Some of them don't like children. Some of them either don't like those kids or they need all the attention themselves. And if they need all the attention, how could they give attention?

My daughter is in the seventh grade and I don't know whether it's her age or what, but she's not too happy with school either. She's more in with whether this teacher likes her, whether the teacher likes the other person, or if so and so gets picked to do certain things and they belong to another group that she doesn't belong to. You can't help it if the teacher likes so and so more than she likes so and so, but it's not only favoritism, it's how there are so many groups now and before we used to be one unit. You would teach the same thing to the whole class. Of course, there were slower children and many who didn't learn and there were a lot of problems, but now because of all the different programs—I'm not saying whether they are good or bad because I haven't been able to see what has each one accomplished—but now it's like everybody is doing their own thing. There are so many alternatives. There's no coordination and no follow-up.

Everything is spur of the moment. It's like saying—I remember, I remember this from my childhood—when my older brother used to like bread he would say, "Oh, I could eat that whole loaf." So my father, to get him out of that, said, "Okay, you like bread? Go ahead and buy yourself a loaf of bread." So then my brother was so happy when he got that loaf of bread and he kept on eating it, but he couldn't eat it all. Okay, so then my father said, "Now you eat it; that's what you wanted." And that's the type of thing I think that they're doing. They say, "Okay, you want community control, and you wanted this and you wanted that. Here. But we're not going to be responsible for it." But they're not really giving it completely because whenever they want they interfere with the community.

There's a lot that I could perceive from the outside and a lot that I have my own feelings about. If something doesn't work—like in machinery, when the machine keeps on doing things that are not quite what you expect it to be doing—you find out what is the cause of it and work from there, but not see something go wrong over and over and over and over again and sit back and not do anything. Because you have the same problems over and over again and you have the same kind of programs over and over again. You know, people that live in the community are so eager that everybody cares, but putting it from the institution's point of view, I don't think they really care. The people that are in the institution, the teachers, principal, the Board of Education, they only care about the institution and that's it.

Black history came during the time that I was working in the school and then I would work with black culture. I would organize bulletin boards and posters in the rooms and try to get the teachers to understand more about black children and black culture. Some of them didn't know how to react to it. Some of them didn't want to get involved. And some of them just looked at it as if: "Well, here they come again to give us a show." Because some of them really believe that because we are in America and they speak English, we should all be Anglo-Saxon. But we don't really ever see Anglo-Saxons. I could say, "Yes, this is an Anglo-Saxon world," if we were to live together, door to door, and they were to see me and I were to see them, and then I would know what they are all about. But if you look at the communities throughout this city you have the Chinese section, you have the Jewish section, you have the Irish section, you have the Italian section, you have the Puerto Rican section, you have the black section, etcetera. So everything around those kids, what they see, what they touch—all their senses tell them that they do not live in an Anglo-Saxon world.

So I worked as a teacher's aide from February 1, 1976, to June 30, 1977, and now the job is ended because we didn't get re-funded. I would like to try to get a similar job somewhere else, and go at the same time to City University. I like teaching, but I haven't made up my mind that that is really what I want to be. Since I was struggling so much to survive, I never sat down to decide what I would like to be or what to make of my life.

I asked Christina about her experience as a single parent and she described some of the problems she had trying to care for her daughter while having to work. She commented on the absence of day care and wondered how a society can nourish the next generation if it does not provide the basic necessities. She returned fleetingly to this theme at the end of our conversations.

Well, being a single parent—you could deal with it, but sometimes it's hard because you kind of find yourself alone, and sometimes you think, well, you need other people around. But then you don't know who is the right person and who is the wrong person and you end up all by yourself because you don't want to get involved with anybody else.

Elena's father is not around at all; I don't think he even knows where I live. I come from a broken family and when people are together, everything is fine; they play father and they play mother. But once there's a breakup in the family, they continue fighting with each other and forget about being a parent, being a mother and a father. Then we get into the cycle where the kid goes here and goes there and doesn't know who or what to believe, and being that my husband and I didn't agree on everything I didn't want to have that extra burden of his telling me, "You can't do this and you can't do that." And since he wasn't giving me any support, I chose to move and I told him where to go. She was five months old. I figured if I'm going to live with somebody or get married to somebody it's going to be for better, not for worse. For worse, I'll stay by myself. But you know, she still asks about him and she always tells me, "Why did you split?" And I try to explain that if you don't agree and things don't work out, you shouldn't live together if you're not going to be happy together. It's hard but I'm more stable now than before.

Before, I didn't have an apartment and I used to work and had to leave her with somebody to take care of her and I had to pay a tremendous amount of money for the child care. But I said, "I brought her to this world and I'm not going to give her up." Then later on I got a three-room apartment on the Lower East Side and had the bathroom in the kitchen and things like that, but at least it was my apartment. I used to take her home Friday nights until Sunday and then leave her with the baby sitter during the week. When she was three or four she told me, "Oh, mommy, I'm grown up, I'm big. You take me with you. You could just leave the milk in the refrigerator and then I'll wait for you." So then I said okay; I didn't do it but I told her we will do it.

It wasn't till I put her into school that I was able to keep her with me most of the time. And then, I would get somebody else to pick her up from school and wait for me. That's why, you know, there should be a way, because, I mean, a society would not be a society without people and they don't provide for the people. A lot of people here don't want to have children; young people are into the thing of not having children. I don't know whether that's right or wrong, that's their own thing, but if a child is born there's got to be some provision.

Oh, when I was a kid, I wanted to have twelve children. Well, at that time my father was working and my mother would be home. My father never wanted my mother to work; even though he earned very little, he didn't want her to work, because the thing was you were poor, but it wasn't the kind of poor where everything was dirty. Everything was pride, you know. He used to come home and he would provide, even though we didn't have a fancy home like some have here—a mansion and three acres of land—but that was our home.

But I always thought that I didn't want to be like my mother and only stay home. I figured the woman had to be, yes, a mother and a wife, but needed to do something else in society—whatever it was—and then come home. I didn't know how I was going to do that, but I thought that my children will grow up and they'll become this and they'll become that. So, then what happened? I was sent over here, and I think that probably changed it. And then I still said, "Oh I want to get married," but I never married so that a husband would take care of me. I always felt that a woman had to have a role just the same way as a man, though I don't know how I was going to accomplish that.

Because you see I don't see any difference between a woman's capacity to achieve and a man's. But I don't think women's liberation is burning your bra or not letting somebody put in the chair for you, and I don't think it's not getting married or having three men if you want to—that's your own thing. Of course, people have to be brought up from very little to believe in this, and now since everybody has been miseducated, they have to be educated, re-educated, about certain things— like they say a woman cannot do certain jobs. There are many jobs that men have that I wouldn't want to do either, because I don't think they're fit for a human being. It's not that type of a thing. It's that a woman should be able to use her capacity and use it to a good purpose and have the same kind of benefit. And let her choose what she wants; if she wants to be a doctor, let that role be open. If she doesn't want to be a doctor, that's it. But let it be for the both of them. And then whoever wants it will become a doctor if they have the capacity to do it. There are plenty of women that can be mothers and there are plenty of ways that a father plays that role. The society has to give the opportunity both to men and women to choose what they want to become. We must be open—open doors, not close them.

You know, in my job when the men used to come around, they would sit there and bullshit. They didn't hardly work at all; they're all drinking coffee or talking about their dreams. But the pitiful part is that dreams take a lot of money, and men—I mean ordinary men—dream but don't have the money. That's why a woman becomes a little more of an economist than a man. Men don't worry so much; they like to dream and to spend and to play their sexist role, but women—because they want to be independent, because they know that they get stuck with the children—they have to plan. Men already have what they call their independence and they don't have to worry. They get married and the wife has the kid and gets stuck with the kid, but men still play that single role. But when the bills come, then they realize that they're not independent either.

We talked about Puerto Rico and New York. Christina has been back and forth many times. I asked her how she felt about each place, if she felt she "belonged" either here or there. And, finally, what kind of a life did she want for her daugher? (While we talked about these topics, Elena was lying on the couch watching television with the aid of an ear plug so that the sound wouldn't disturb her mother and me. She seemed totally absorbed in a game show in which the prizes were lavish vacations, cars, and large amounts of money.)

In Puerto Rico when you wake up in the morning you see the whole horizon, green with flowers, and you see the dew and you hear the birds or the animals. It's aliveness. And, even though it's not yours, you hear a radio or you hear voices or you hear dishes crinkling. Over here—oh, for Christ's sake, this place looks so ugly. Because I can look out the window, I feel a little better. I can see the front, but a lot of people live in the back. So what do you see? You see the clothes hanging down. In Puerto Rico you see the sky or you see, far away, the mountains. Over here you see the window at night with the gate. This looks like a prison, grayish. In Puerto Rico mostly everybody has the house painted pink or green. Here you feel like—like you're being punished. Like you get taken from there and you get put in here with no windows to look out, and you feel like a prisoner.

When we came here, five of us had to live in a basement with two rooms, and I said, "This is ridiculous. How could we live?" If you have three rooms in a tropical country, it seems like more because you're around a lot of children and a lot of people and you have the outdoors. You can open the windows and you can see and it doesn't enclose your mind, so you dream up tremendous ideas. Over here you can't dream.

The older people, they belong there. They are always talking about Puerto Rico; that's their home and they will go back and buy a house and live over there. The children don't know where they belong because really they weren't there that long. The older people were raised there. They had a life; they had a home; they know how to go back and forth. But the children don't belong. They feel like they don't belong here and they don't know how to go back and forth.

After Elena was born, I went to Puerto Rico and I tried working over there, but being that I have already worked over here, have lived over here since I was a kid, I didn't like the life there. First of all I wasn't earning that much money and I was working these tremendous hours, and I was living with my mother, which I didn't really want to do. I wanted to live on my own—not break away completely from them—but I wanted to be my own person. I could go and visit them, they could come visit me, but I didn't want to depend on them. So I decided to come back. They didn't have the programs there that they have here and the mobility to find other jobs. And there's a lot of male chauvinism there. Oh God, over there the wives are in the house, taking care of children, and if a woman goes out alone she gets criticized from the family and from the men. Right away they figure, well, this woman is looking for something.

What do I want for my daughter? Well, she has her own ideas already. She wants to go back to Puerto Rico. That's because my mother's there. Because my mother's always dreaming about Puerto Rico, the kids tend to take on the dream. I tell her that I want her to, let's say, study and she can become whatever she wants to become. I don't want her to be stuck in a sense that she has to take up my dreams or my mother's dream. Let her do her own dreams. The older people have lived their life already; but children coming from different backgrounds, different experiences, have to make their own adjustments. I don't want her to be obligated to the old because . . . you know . . . my father was a big dreamer and he's still a big dreamer. He always dreamed of the independence of Puerto Rico, right? But sometimes mothers and fathers, they have their dreams and the children are forgotten. They're not practical in the sense that if you're the mother and the father and you don't take care of your kids, how are they going to grow up to become part of that dream? I'm not saying that it's easy; I'm not doing the best job in the world either.

Because of my experience of going back and forth, my solution is not to dream at all—and just do—because life changes. My experience was that they sent me over here—for whatever reason. Even if they told me today why I got sent here, it still does something to you, to your mind—makes you believe and not believe—you know that things can change abruptly.

My mother was into the dream of buying a house and my father was into the dream of independence and then you have the children. And they tell you; become this and this and that. But you're not doing it, right? How the hell do I know how to do it? Like in the school, if they tell you that you have to wear a gym suit and you have to wear the sneakers and you have to do this and you have to do that, that takes money. Or they have to take you to the doctor; that takes money. Maybe they couldn't do it because they didn't have the money. They tell you you got to go out there and study, but at the same time, either because they can't or because they don't want to or they're too tied up with their dreams, they don't help you. They just want you to do and expect you to figure it out yourself.

Even on television, they plan you out. Now they have single parents, but before it was a family. So and so was a doctor and so and so was a PTA president. The kids grow up and they're going to college. But you say, how do they do it? They don't tell you how they get there. They assume, then you assume—but how *do* they get there? And where did they get the money? And how come they have money and we don't have money? All those questions, but a kid doesn't ask those questions. They assume that everything is there, that the money is there, that there is a money tree or something. They don't want to realize that it costs you money to live. Because the city doesn't supply anything. It doesn't supply you with a fruit, with a banana, it doesn't even supply you with a mango.

CHAPTER 3

Diane DiMarco

I know my job inside out. They put down a piece of paper; I pick it up; I type it. No thinking.

When we met for the first time, Diane was wearing a mauve jersey nightgown. Our appointment was scheduled for early one Saturday morning, but Diane had overslept so she talked with me for the next two hours sitting cross-legged on her couch in her nightgown, smoking long cigarillos. She is a small, slim, twenty-three-year-old woman with short, blond, wavy hair, a heart-shaped face, brown eyes, and a cleft in her chin.

Diane lives in a fifty- or sixty-year-old, freestanding apartment building on a service road beside a major highway. Her building is on the fringe of a busy, working-class neighborhood, but it is isolated and run down. Nearby are a few stores and a movie house that shows erotic films.

The entryway of Diane's building is dark, but the hallways on the upper floors are brighter and more cheerful. The living room of her three-room apartment is large with high ceilings but nevertheless very dark. Diane has painted the walls light blue and planned that the room would be primarily blue, black, and silver. Along one wall is a long, black naughahyde couch with a modern stainless-steel lamp beside it; a black, wrought-iron table and chairs are in a corner; and a television set and stereo equipment are along the wall opposite the couch.

Diane comes from an Italian family and is a clerical worker for a large public utility. She is single. While her talk is rapid and "hip," she has an air of openness and warmth and often seems extraordinarily vulnerable.

I don't know how to start. Should I start about how I started living here? I've been living here less than a year and I hate it. It's kind of old and dingy. I feel I can't fix it up the way I want to because—look at how it is. I would love a modern apartment, but the reason I took this apartment was because I was in a rush to get out of my house so I grabbed the first one that I could find.

I was living in a beautiful house about eight blocks away with my brother who is thirty, but we don't get along too good, you know. The house was left to us. See, my father was a gambler and he got arrested and he's been in jail since I was fifteen. Then my mother stayed with us—like, it was me, my sister, my brother, and my mother in a beautiful house. When my mother and my father were together, it was, like, a perfect little family. My father really spoiled us, like, he'd give us everything. He had money but when he got in trouble just about all of his money went to lawyers because he tried desperately not to go to jail. While he was away, my sister got married. She's a beautiful person; she's strictly, like, you know, mother and housewife. She has it all together. She lives in a beautiful section of the Bronx in a beautiful, beautiful house. She's really got it together; she knows what she wants and she did it—the right way. My brother got married late, just last year, and they just had a little baby girl. Now he has the house with his wife.

See, my mother, she started working, and after a while, after my father was away, I mean—he's away for seven years now, that's a long time—so one time my brother saw her walking with a man and he, like, flipped out because we're very close with my father. So she had to pack up, she cut out of the house, cause my brother's very strict and he carried on to no end, so she split. One morning I just woke up and there was no one at the table. I had no idea of what was going on. I was only nineteen at the time. And ever since then me and my brother kept up the house, but we didn't get along, not at all. Like, we're still very close now that I'm not living with him, but to live with him, we just don't get along. So, that's how I got this apartment.

My mother just got remarried during the summer. Since my father was away, she got a divorce right away. They mailed him the papers telling him that she's divorced from him and then she met this other man who I know and she married him just this summer. And I went to her wedding. I figured, she's got her own life, too; she's human. I'm not too friendly with her. I'm really only friendly with her because of her part. Like, you know, she gives me a lot, and she'll always call me, she'll always invite me over. Like, it sounds as if she's saying, "Oh, anything for my daughter." But I don't consider myself a phony person, and when she left I had just turned nineteen. I was out of high school in June, I turned nineteen in July. I had just started working. My brother doesn't work; he, like, plays cards—that's his life. And, you know, they have their bad times and their good times.

When my mother left in September, I was having a terrible problem with this guy that I know, this guy that I still love. And I had just broken off my engagement with this other guy who could have offered me everything. I broke off my engagement and then it went from there; I was having terrible trouble. Like, I was brought up right. I'm your girlfriend—you're my boyfriend. You know what I mean? But Tony was a whole different story. He came from Manhattan. I met him at work. And I was so stupid, so sincere. From the very beginning I flipped out over this guy. I had been going with another guy for over two years—I was engaged to him, I had my wedding hall, everything. My mother gave us a big engagement party. I met Tony and in less than a month I broke off my engagement. And still, to this day, I'm crazy about him. It was so strong. And then I was having trouble with him. Too many things happened at once.

When she left, I had to pay the mortgage and everything. You see, my brother would help me, but he is a gambler and sometimes he would even ask me for money to go and play cards. It was impossible. I got myself in a terrible jam because I started paying for everything, but I was young and I wanted to go out, too. I wanted to go places—dances, everything—so I got these credit cards. And what I would do is buy my clothes and everything on credit cards and the rest of my money would go for bills. I really never had any spending money so I took the credit cards and charged everything and couldn't pay them and now my credit is destroyed—I mean really bad. And I was just starting out. Even now I only bring home about a hundred and sixty dollars. I make two hundred and forty-three dollars gross, which is good, and I'm taking home a hundred and sixty dollars so you can imagine four years ago I wasn't even taking home that much. I started my job making a hundred and nine dollars a week. The mortgage was very low, but every year I had to pay like two hundred dollars for house insurance, and you know gas and electric is very high on a house.

And, like, he was very strict with me. I could be all dressed up, ready to go out, and he would walk in and, like, he wanted me to vacuum the rugs, clean the room—he actually wanted me to play the role of my mother. I used to tell him, "I know I'm not keeping up the house that great, but you got to understand that I work all week and I'm young—on the weekends I want to go out." We had a lot of conflicts about that. I used to tell him, "I'm not your wife, and I'm not your mother. I'm just like you in this house. You know I got a bad break too." And, oh boy, we used to fight about that. He'd come in and say, "Don't I have clean undershirts?" And I used to get smacked and stuff like that. But I always answered back.

You see, when my mother left, my sister and I became very, very close and I became very dependent on her. She's only twenty-five, but she holds the family together. So when my brother got married I said, "Look, you need your own privacy so I'm going to move down to the basement." So my brother said, "All right." My sister came over on the weekend and she says, "I'll help you." And my brother starts to tease me about my cat. I had a little kitten and refused to give it up. And we had two dogs in the house and he would always let the dogs run after it. I didn't think it was funny, but he would let the dogs out and laugh, right? But I used to get mad. So I caught the dog and I took her out front; I told her, "Go ahead, get out." And I went upstairs and I said, "If you want your dog, she's outside."

Now, this little dog, she's crazy. She's running in the streets. She was, like, really wild. Well, he had such a fit that he came running down, and picked up this big trash can that I had been using to get rid of all the junk I didn't want and throws it all in the kitchen, right? And he starts yelling—like he got into one of his fits—and my sister had her little son there. She had never seen one of his fits; she only heard about them. When he went upstairs she told me, "You better pack your clothes. I'm picking you up tomorrow." But I was afraid of my brother. I said, "No. No. He'll kill me." She said, "No, he won't. I'll come and get you." I was crying hysterically, crying, "Please help me, I can't live with him no more," and she did. She came the next day and when I left, instead of my brother being mad, he felt really bad—like he cried, you know. I guess he figured we had lived together so long we depended on each other and I guess he really felt bad. And ever since then, we've been getting along great.

I don't like this apartment, but I would never go back home. Never. It doesn't bother me to live alone. You know what my biggest fear is? Getting robbed, because if they take this, this is all I got. I do want to get another lock on my door because of that, not because there's a very mixed crowd in here. There's a good amount of blacks, but people mind their own business—nobody's even approached me. I only know two families in the building. But the good thing about it is that the candy store downstairs, the guy that owns it is an Italian so that at a certain time each night I think maybe they play numbers—I'm not sure—but I know that at a certain time in the night there's all these Italian men sitting out there and I feel safe then. Sometimes I just pass and say hi. I don't talk to them but it makes me feel safe.

I'm not afraid, but when my mother came up here she was, like, a nut; she was scared. She made a big scene over it. And when my mother carries on like that that's when I resent her. I feel like telling her, "If you were worried about me years ago, I wouldn't be here now." I really resent her. I have to say it. Like, I love her, I love to buy her nice gifts, but I do resent her. I just wish that she'd be a mother like a mother should be. My brother and sister would like a nice fat Italian mother and if you should see her, she's definitely not that. She's fifty years old but you'd never believe it. She looks better than me.

Everybody always knew that my father and I were close. Every year when I got my income tax money, when other girls would go out and spend it on clothes or on their apartments, I would always take my income tax money and go down to Atlanta and visit my father. This is the first year I haven't gone, but I intend on going. I've flown down there so many times. He's afraid to let me sleep over so he only lets me stay one day.

For about a year or two he was down here in Lower Manhattan because he was brought up on another case, and we had so much fun.

Now you know I'm always broke. It seems like ever since my mother left, even though I have a dynamite job, I'm always broke. My mother will do things for me, but she won't really, really go out of her way. But my father, not every time but once in a while when he was in prison here, he would give me a hundred-dollar bill and I'd say, "Dad, where did you get that?" When I go to see him, people think I'm his girlfriend, 'cause, like, I'm all over him and he's all over me. I sit on his lap and we hug each other and I'll play with his hair. He's, like—like dynamite. He's so great I wish he would live forever. I really do. He's supposed to come home this April or May. Isn't that great? I can't wait, you have no idea. I know that all of our lives—my brother's, my sister's, and mine—are going to be different. I know that mine is. I know I'm going to have better days. You need somebody that you know loves you, 'cause otherwise I would feel like I had nobody. I would never go to my mother. I could be starving and I would never go to her.

When I met Diane, she had just broken up once again with Tony and was eager to talk about him. Her relationships with men—her father, her brother, the man to whom she was engaged before she met Tony, and especially Tony—seem to be pivotal, literally those around which her life revolves and evolves, while women almost seem to be supporting characters.

Okay, so Tony worked where I work, but in the field. He came up to the office for an accident report and that's how I first met him. I guess he noticed me. I was leaving early that day and I was taking the steps because I was in a rush, I remember, and he ran down the steps right behind me and started saying, "What's your name?" and I was walking down and I was saying, "Diane." And he goes, "Mine is Tony." I go, "Hi." He goes, "You work upstairs? Who do you work for?" I was answering him, but I didn't even really look at him. Just when I got to the lobby he said, "Hey, are you married?" I turned around and said, "No." That's when I looked at him and I thought he was

kind of cute, you know. And ever since then, every day when he would pull up into the garage or whatever, he would come upstairs and say hello and stop and ask me out and I would never go out with him, right? And I told him I was engaged and all this and he said, "Yeah, I know. I know." He probably asked one of his friends in the office about me.

He would call me at work all the time and then for about two or three days I didn't see him at all and after about a week of him coming every day, I missed him. You know, like I says, "Oh wow, see, I lost that guy." Right? So the next time he came up, I was talking on the phone to John, my boyfriend, and I looked up and I said, "Oh, I have to go now to do something for my boss." That's how happy I was to see him. And then he says, "So when are we going out?" And then I says, "All right, I'll go out with you," 'cause I knew I missed him.

So I went out with Tony and I liked him and then he would drive me home from work every day. So we got involved just like that and then I was getting sick because I was young and like I would be in the car with Tony and we would park for about an hour and I would be talking with him, kissing him and everything. Then I would go to John's house and, like, John would start kissing me. I couldn't handle it. I was about eighteen-and-a-half and it was bothering me, you know. And on the weekends I couldn't see Tony at all; I could just call him because he gave me his number. And then I broke off with John.

It was two weeks after I was seeing him that I found out he was Spanish, 'cause he never told me and he looked Italian. He just said to me, "Are you Italian?" and I said, "Yeah," and he says, "Oh." Someone had mentioned to me in the office that he was Spanish. I asked him that day and he just laughed, but by then I didn't care. And then he took me by his neighborhood, 138th, between Broadway and Amsterdam, and I was so petri- fied. He says, "I'm just going to check the mail box." I says, "No, no, you're not leaving me in this car." He says, "You want to come?" I says, "No." So he says, "All right, I'll get one of my friends to stay with you." He calls this Spanish guy with a big Afro. I was so scared.

The first time he took me up to his house I was, like, you

know, looking all around. I was so amazed at it. He had five rooms, right? And the bathroom when I walked in was just a bathroom. No curtains, no drapes, no rugs, you know, just the sink, the tub, and the bowl. And the kitchen had a little table in it and an old linoleum, and the living room had no furniture in it and I think he had it painted red with black trimming. His room was nice. Now I'll say it's nice because I've gotten used to it, but when I first saw his room, you know, it was just pieces of furniture, like, odds and ends. It was something I wasn't used to because all I knew was our house and when my mother lived there our house was gorgeous. I was so shocked and, like, my heart went out to him in a way. You know, I thought he was a ghetto child. But meanwhile the guy was happy; he thought he had himself hooked up. An apartment, a job, a car. But I didn't care 'cause for some reason or other, I was in another world over him.

Another big thing was in the beginning, when I went out with him, he was, like, very experienced at sex—I guess because he was on his own in Manhattan from about fifteen. When I met him he must have been about twenty-one. And I wasn't experienced. Even though I was engaged to John, it was, like, just like, you know, how you fool around and stuff like that, right? But I wasn't a virgin. Okay. Well, the first night that I was with Tony nothing was even accomplished. I was totally froze-up. You know, it was just useless. But he was cool. He just, like, watched TV and then we went to sleep and, you know, we had a really nice night. But then eventually, I got it right and I was amazed at him. I was thoroughly amazed the first night that I had sex with him because it was really experiencing sex, you know, to the fullest. And I was, like, freaked out over it. It was a very long time before it could wear off.

And then my mother left and I had broke up with Tony at the same time because I thought that I was his girl, you know, that's how I was brought up, but I started seeing hickeys on his neck and these girls would be calling the house, 'cause I was getting so familiar that I was staying there without him and I'd answer the phone. Or, I'd call him up from my house early in the morning and a girl would answer. Finally after about eight or

nine months of that—I liked him so much that it would just kill me—I couldn't put up with a situation like that. I says, "Look, I have to leave you," and I did.

He used to come around and call and everything, but I totally ignored him. Then we made up and I told him, "I'll live with you so that you can be with somebody every day because I don't trust you." So I started living with him and going home, like, two nights a week to clean the house for my brother, do the laundry. And I was still paying the rent on the house. During that time, it was, like, the greatest five months of a relationship. Every day we'd go to work together, come home. We'd cook; we'd start to fix up the house—I was totally happy. You know, that's when I left my family because I didn't even care, I was so happy. I didn't think of nothing else.

Then he lost his job and everything got screwed up. He got caught by the city police stealing cable from the company. He lost his job and he got probation. Okay, then I found a set of works in one of his drawers. I found a syringe and a cooker, and it was all wrapped up in a rubber band. And his sister came in the room. She's a real bitch, you know, so she told me, "Oh yeah, that's another thing about my brother"—like, she always used to put him down—"sometimes he gets high with his friend next door." But in the meantime, when I was very young, I used to mess around with pills, and we would, say, snort dope and stuff like that. So, about a week later, I noticed he was high, or I came home and caught them getting high or something, I don't remember. And I says, "What's this?" and he got all upset and everything. And I just glanced over it and said, "Don't worry," and I got high with them. He didn't want me to, there was a big argument, but the guy that he was with says, "Oh, come on, we'll skin it," and I said, "Tony, I've done it before," and he looked upset and we went through a whole big hassle, but I did it, and then I guess since I went along with it it was easier for him just to bring it out in the open and then that's when we started getting into drugs.

Then he started, not really dealing dope, but he was a good connection and he was making a lot of money on that, tons of money. But he would get a lot of dope for free. So that's how we were getting over. And then, of course, he met with guys in the street and they started—they taught him how to pick locks, right? And they said, "You know you could make a lot of money with B and Es* and everything, right?" We were loaded. Thoroughly loaded.

The only thing I have definitely to say good about this guy is he never took a penny from me. But he used to take money from other girls. This one girl used to put me through hell. When he was in jail, Tony told me that he used to go to bed with her and she used to always give him money. And she was, like, trampy and everything. And it used to bug me—like, "How could you be with that girl?" Like, I felt so clean and spotless next to her. Just to look at her—It used to really bug me 'cause no girls that I ever found out about were gorgeous. They were all, like, maybe black, and I mean not attractive black girls, just a regular black girl, and it used to turn me off very much. I used to say, "Tony, why?" Like, you know, "You have me, you never complain about me, what do you see in them?" I used to get nuts over this.

He really gave me a complex. And I was looking good then. I was even thinner because I was getting high and when I get high, I'm very into myself. Like, right after I get high, I'll go wash my face and put my makeup on. I'll blow out my hair. Unless I was really stoned, nobody would ever believe that I got high because of how I looked. I was very self-conscious. I would lose weight, make sure I had a good figure. Never walked around in a housecoat with my hair dirty, never. And I would learn how to dance; if he took me out I would be able to dance dynamite and hustle and all that and yet, I thought I was really not so fantastic. Like, I really felt, that maybe I was too slow for him, or nice but not cool enough, right? I was constantly worried.

Then one time I got busted with him; that was an experience, too. He had a lot of tools and he had this big pipe cutter. Now, me, not that I'm brave or anything, I guess I'm just dumb and I'm not, like, afraid of anything. I wanted to be his partner,

---

* Breaking and entering.

not just his girlfriend. I didn't want to just be thrown in the house to be used as his girlfriend. Everything he did I could get into. And his friends dug me. They figured I was dynamite, 'cause I wasn't a chick that would go out and say, "Oh, it's cold out." Me, I'd hung out on the corner with them, you know, get things together, help them out tremendously. Like, they all would do anything for me. So when he used to go anywhere, I used to worry about him and I always felt if I was there, I knew I would help him, knew I would watch his back. Of course, he used to argue with me about it, but I always used to get my way no matter what.

So we used to cut the meters, like, say, the quarter meters and then we used to bring them home, break the pins in there and get the money out and you'd get thirty or forty dollars out of one meter. And we'd take a few of them. So one night he wanted to get high; we had no money; and I was upset and a little depressed and he was getting nuts now that he wanted to get high. I said, "Tony, we don't have the money. We're not going to get high tonight." For some reason or other, I don't know, I sensed something—and I'm very superstitious and I didn't want to go. He says, "Look, I'm going to go out and get some money." I said, "No. No, don't go out." He said, "I'm going whether you go or not." So I said, "No, I'll go with you." But I didn't want to go so I took so long to get dressed and he was getting pissed off. So I said, "Tony, I don't want to go out there tonight."

But we went out, just me and him. We had a shopping cart and everything and we were copping meters and I was looking out. Now a cab had parked, which I didn't even notice, 'cause at the time cops had just started riding around in yellow cabs. So the two cops, they were dressed in, like, army uniforms—they looked Spanish, and I saw them from all the way down the corner, just walking, talking, and I don't know why, I just sensed it. I go, "Tony, stop." He goes, "Why, what's the matter?" I go, "Stop, just wait until those two guys down there come up the block and go." He says, "I'm not worried about them, man," 'cause they really looked like regular guys. I go, "Would you just stop?"—real upset. Sure enough he stops. We're standing there talking. He's annoyed, of course. Sure enough they were just walking up the block and when they just about reach us they turn around and they each grab one of us by the arm and said, "You're under arrest." I said, "Oh, my God, I don't believe this!" They took us in the cab and there was a girl there, too, who I didn't get along with at all, a girl that works with them, a black girl.

They brought us to the 125th Street Station and it was the first time I was busted, and I started screaming and yelling. So I was carrying on and they were getting really annoyed with me. And Tony was begging me, "Please, shut up, because that black girl doesn't like you and she wants to keep you here all night. Don't let that happen to me—I don't want to see you here all night; I'll go nuts." Of course, I didn't know any better; I was never in jail at night. I had blond hair and it was long at the time and it's a good thing I didn't stay over.

There was an Italian lieutenant there and he came up, and boy he was pissed off at me. He picked up my sheet and he looked at it, and he seen all the Italian names, you know, my father's, my mother's, real Italian names, and he started yelling at me. "What are you, a junkie?" I says, "No, I'm not a junkie." And of course I was nasty because I was embarrassed; the guy was right, you know.

So, then I had to go in the next room and I had to strip right down to my underclothes in front of this black girl; she was checking us to see if we had dope or weapons. I was so afraid. I didn't want them to know I was getting high, and I was so afraid she was going to see my arms but the way I did everything was so cool that she didn't see my arms. She did a good job on me but she didn't touch me.

And they did the same to Tony inside, and then they score you on points. And of course I didn't know anything about it. Now I'm really scared, saying, "Oh God, they're going to keep me all night." Now I'm calm, I'm quiet because the black guy up there says, "Honey, you better be cool, 'cause I would hate to see you spend the night in jail." Like, he was real nice to me. He said, "Just be quiet. You're busted anyway; it ain't worth it, you know." Now I started crying. Either I'm mad or I cry. I didn't know then that they had no chance to keep me there really because I had never been busted. I was a working girl; I had a completely good record. Tony got out because he lied; he said he was still working.

When we went back to court, he took the weight of stealing from me and they gave him probation. In other words, he said I was just standing around, that I had nothing to do with it.

So then one Monday morning I remember I was laying in bed and I knew he was inside making breakfast for me. He made me eggs and steak, the whole bit, you know. And I was very uneasy that morning and so was he and I just looked at him. I said, "What's the matter?" And he started crying. The first time I saw him crying; this upset me totally, you know. He started crying and telling me that he was very unhappy with the way he was living—stealing and everything. He said he would do anything to get his job back and be like it was. And when I left, he says, "Look I have to go out and make money today. I'm going to try and straighten out, but until I do, you know I've got to pay my rent and everything." I said, "Look, just be careful. Keep in touch with me at work." And I was upset all day because I remember telling this guy that I'm very close with, I says, "I'm so worried about him. I know something's going to happen to him." I said, "I don't know what it's going to be but I know it's pretty soon."

And sure enough, that afternoon Tony got busted. See, his friend Bob had a gun and he used to carry it with him every place they had to go and this used to make me sick. Always had to have that damn gun. They were doing a *B* and *E* and they were going into this apartment and trying to get into the front door, and this lady was coming in, this older lady, she was about fifty-six years old, and she's talking to them and she's saying, "Oh, are you going to the super also to pay the rent?" So of course Bob looks at Tony as if to say we could rip her off, she's got rent money on her.

So this is the story I get from them, I don't know how true it is. I never got the true story, I wasn't there. Tony didn't want to do that. He didn't want to mess with people. But Bob figured this was fast and easy so he just said, "Tony, I'm doing it. I'm doing it." He said to the old lady, "Listen, Miss, we ain't here to pay our rent. Give the rent money, right?" She looked at them and she wouldn't give it. And then Bob took out his gun and he pointed the gun at her and this is supposedly the story. She wouldn't give it up. He says, "Lady, are you crazy? Give up your money, I have a gun to your head." And Tony kept saying, "Bob, come on, I'm cutting out, I'm cutting out." Bob says, "I'm angry we don't have the money." And he went to grab it from her and out of being upset or nervous or whatever, the gun went off and it shot her, like, in the back, by her behind. The two of them started running, and just as they ran out of the building, Bob threw the gun and they both were running in different directions and a cop car came along just then. The cops saw them running and they heard the lady screaming for help and they caught the both of them. Right there. And they found the gun, the whole bit.

I left work, of course, and I went to that precinct. I never saw him again outside. Then he went to Riker's Island and I used to go see him every day for about two weeks. Then we went to court and he got a zero- to three-year sentence and then they told him he would have to do ten months in prison before he goes in front of the Parole Board and then when he went in front of the Board I think they hit him with another six months. He did eighteen months altogether. And then they let him out.

So what happened to me was that I totally broke down. I was very upset, a nervous wreck, so I went to a doctor. I was still getting high but the doctor didn't know this. I went to him and my arms were clean cause I was getting off in a different place where it wasn't noticeable, right? And he told me that I was a nervous wreck and that I should calm down. It was like a day or two after Tony got busted and he gave me Valiums, and he put me off work about ten days. So I was taking the Valiums three times a day and I was going to Riker's Island every day to see Tony.

After a week I was very thin. I practically didn't eat. My clothes were just hanging on me. I looked terrible; I was crying, the whole bit. Now what happened was my father got shipped from Georgia to New York for a case and as soon as he got here, he made a call and everybody went down to see him. He wanted to know where his daughter was, right? So my sister says, "Look, Dad, I'm going to tell you a story," 'cause he never knew I was living with Tony. But my sister I never lied to, except for the drugs. She told him the whole story. He said, "Go and get her. Tell her I'm not angry with her. Everything is cool. Tell her I want to see her."

My sister came to where I was living. She picked me up. She was hysterical crying when she saw where I was living. She freaked out over it. She says, "Get all your things, pack up everything." So I went to see my father and oh, do I look terrible! I was crying all the way downtown. I was scared too. So I looked bad. And when he saw me—and he always used to see me looking so pretty, 'cause when I'd go to see him, you know how you get all extra-special dolled-up—I think he started crying. Not really crying but, like, he just kept looking at me, and saying, "Baby, what happened?" I was hysterical crying. And, like, I told him the whole story, right? And, like, he just says, "Your creepy brother. You pay the rent? You're still paying the rent?" Of course he called up my brother and 'cause of the things he said to my brother, my brother didn't talk to him for about a month.

And I would go see my father then, every weekend. I was getting myself together. I got off the Valiums, I went back to work, I was taking care of myself again, and I was still seeing Tony. My father would tell me, "I don't want you going to no prisons. You had enough with me, right?" He says, "I don't want you going through it with this guy, you're not married to him." So I says, "Yeah, all right." But of course I didn't listen. One day I would go see my father on the weekend, the other day I'd go see Tony. But it was too much for me to handle. My brother was hassling me, my father was driving me, I was running like a nut upstate to see Tony, down to see my father. I couldn't handle it; I was very depressed. Then I met this guy, Jimmy, a very nice looking guy; he was also into drugs. I started going out with him and so eventually I left Tony. And he knew it and everything and he was brokenhearted over it. And I never forgave myself for that.

I started getting high again with Jimmy. He lost his job. I

felt I was hard luck, you know. Now, I'm thoroughly disgusted—I'm getting high again, Jimmy is getting high again, right? Money was bad 'cause I was getting high and then eventually I broke off with him and I was still getting high and I was constantly depressed about Tony. Because any guy I met could never hold my interest, I used to constantly say, only Tony was the one. And it was over; I'll never see him again.

He got out in August of '76 and I knew he was out because every once in a while I would run into people and they'd say they seen him. I was hanging out, going to clubs, and everytime I was in Manhattan, I'd check out all the clubs, 'cause I figured he'd need a job, he knew all the owners, he'd be bartendering. I was always afraid that I would run into him, paranoid about what I'd say if he's with another girl. It would break my heart, you know. So I was getting high and hanging out with my friends, right? Now I was getting high every day, without fail, on my own, getting up the money, that's how I messed up. I would wake up, spend the day at work, and straight from work about four of us, after our jobs—we all had jobs—we would all meet, we'd go over to one of our apartments, get high, party out. That's what it was about, every night. So one day I'm at work and Tony calls me up and I was shocked. I started crying, hysterical, I said, "Wow, forgive me." Like, the whole scene. "I want to see you tonight" and everything. And I had this apartment; there was hardly nothing in it, a few pieces of furniture, not painted, or nothing. So, I gave him the address and he came up.

Now, I couldn't get high that night so I came right home. I dressed up; I fixed myself up nice. I didn't want him to see my arms, I wore long sleeves. I made myself look really good so that he wouldn't know. I don't know if he sensed it or what, but we were talking on the couch and at first I was crying, like a whole hour, carrying on. And then he saw my arms. Because I was making marks on my arms and the summer was coming and I was worried about the job, I cleared them up but then I was getting high in my wrists, and of course, he saw the marks 'cause he knew what to look for. So that night because I didn't get high I was up all night. The next night I couldn't sleep either. And you can't just lay down. You feel like your bones inside are cracking, and you've got to get up and walk around. I had this big problem with my legs; it was flipping me out. I'd get up, I'd take two aspirins. Get up again, take another two. The third night, with the aspirins, I got a little bit of sleep. A few hours here and there. The fourth night I was all right; I was so exhausted that I slept good. And I knew then that I was cool, that everything was all right.

He always comes right on time, I'll say the truth about that. I got cleaned up from that and my bills got caught up so everything was fine. I guess I was definitely on my way down, but Tony came right on time. When I did stop, I said, "Wow, thank God this guy came!"

The only thing now is, like, I smoke pot. And when I go partying out with my friends and some guy has ups I'll take an up, and if I'm some place that people have downs, and if everybody's taking them and we're partying maybe I'll take a down. But now I'm not into them; I get smokes. That's it. I'll tell you the truth, as far as the dope goes, I don't have an urge for it at all. I guess because I know where it would lead me. See, last time I got into it it turned into something serious where I wasn't paying my bills. Now, I feel, why get into that when I know I can't handle my apartment and everything. And I think now I'm too old. Before, I was younger so I was hanging out a lot, maybe in the street, on corners, stuff like that. But now I'm older. I would rather just stay home or go to relatives or go out and enjoy myself. You know what I mean? Like, I'm not into just hanging out in parks, hanging out in the streets. I think I just ran through it and I happened to make it. I was very fortunate. I was never in a methadone program; my name was never down for drugs. The only thing I did wrong was when I got busted.

As Diane pointed out, she has avoided serious trouble—with her job, with the law, with drugs—and has therefore avoided contact with human-service intitutions. When I asked her if she had ever thought of getting professional help when she was on drugs she said that she did not feel she really had a habit and therefore did not need help. Yet she was quick to say that it was Tony's calling her and beginning their relationship again that saved her when she was "on her way down." While her social and family network has been partially responsible for some of her problems, that same network has helped her to work things out at each stage: she obtained her current job through her boyfriend; her sister helped her to move into her own apartment; Tony helped her to get off drugs; and her father will be home soon—perhaps to change her life once again.

Her union shop steward has provided the only outside help she has received. When she was using drugs heavily, Diane often found it difficult to get to work on time and when she was repeatedly reprimanded by her boss, her shop steward interceded for her, went with her to meetings with her supervisor and generally smoothed the way. Diane claims that no one at work suspected that she was on drugs. "My boss just used to say, 'Oh, she goes out all the time. She's out late partying and she can't get up in the morning.' "

Diane went on to describe the repetitive and mindless nature of her job and yet the casual, intimate atmosphere that holds her by enabling her to "goof around." She described the sexual pressures on the women in her office and the union's role in protecting these women from sexual coercion by protecting their jobs. But while the union could protect them from sexual harassment directly connected with job security, it could not protect them from more subtle coercion or from the coercive power of money. She pointed out that while being made part of "management" is a promotion, it is at best a mixed blessing since one loses the job security provided by the union and is then considerably more at the mercy of "the boss." The conflict between advancement and job security, between having a job you can "get into" and not needing to be sexually available to the boss, is clear and dramatic. For now, at least, Diane has opted to remain where she is.

I started my job on June 27, 1972, right after I graduated from Catholic high school. How did I feel about school? I was pretty bad, behavior-wise. I was very good marks-wise—like, in anything I didn't have to study for. Anything I had to study for I would fail because I would never study. Now arithmetic you don't study for; you learn in the class. If I ever got less than a ninety on my report card I can't even remember it. Bookkeeping, too, steno, anything you don't have to study for. I know I'm pretty smart; it's just that I was lazy—like, I couldn't be bothered. And I used to fool around a lot, just goof around—I always like to have fun. I guess I was never a serious person.

In my junior year I was very bad: I used to cut classes and play hooky; they would call up my house and my mother was working so I knew I could never get caught. But then they called next door and the guy next door to me, who I eventually got engaged to—he was much older, five years older than me—he called my mother at her job and told her. And I had to go to school with my mother and she got pissed off at me. My father was in jail and she was strict—like, she'd yell and holler and maybe even smack you. And finally, I used to tell her, "I want to go to public school. If I play hooky all the time, I'll get expelled and then you'll have to let me go to public school." I was being really nasty. And she says, "I'll tell your brother." And she told him, but he didn't hit me; and he just said, "You think you're going to public school, huh? You ain't going nowhere." And then, right after that, I started going out with that guy, John, and he straightened me out. In the senior year my marks improved because I was studying—because I was with him. I wasn't going out with friends or anything. I was just going out with him and I graduated with good marks.

And, you know, from when I was, like, fourteen, I wanted to be a hairdresser. People on the block that were going to weddings and stuff—they would say, "Do my hair, do my makeup." I was always into that. And then my mother says, "O.K., I'll send you to hairdressing school straight from high school. This way in six months you'll be finished." And even though she was struggling while my father was away, she knew it would be worthwhile. But John wouldn't let me go. He wouldn't let me go to school 'cause he says I'd be working on the weekends and he'd be working during the week and we were getting married, so what could I say? I was getting married to him. And I was young. And because of that, I'm not a hairdresser.

Then, as soon as I graduated high school, John knew this guy who's a big man in the union and so he helped me get into this company. I went down for the job and I got it because they already knew I was getting it.

So a couple of weeks after I graduated I started the same job I'm doing now; I never transferred or changed. I'm there five-and-a-half years. I answer phones; I have a Call Director with about twelve phones and I do typing for five big bosses and any departments under them. There's another girl, she's management and she works for the general manager, but they give the typing to her too, just like me. She's very good, a black girl; I get along with her fantastic. We type memos, letters to the outside and to interoffice, and sometimes the guys just need favors, like, in other words, they want things typed for their records and files, so we do that, too. A lot of the guys go to school—and we don't have to, but we type up their reports and stuff.

I would never transfer to any other building 'cause it's very formal in all the other buildings. Where I work, for some reason—maybe because it's very small, only ten floors—they're very informal. I could go to work just like this, with these draggy dungarees. It's so informal that it's dynamite. I have so much fun on the job. You get really close to the people; they invite you to their house, even married couples. And, like, a lot of people there smoke pot. Everybody is forever turning each other on. You see somebody high, they'll give you a joint. If you want to borrow money, you could ask even the bosses. Like, everybody plays the numbers together; we pass out the football tickets. It's really, really unbelievable.

I get in so much trouble. I did very bad on the job. I know I have capabilities, like being smart, picking up fast, and that was the only reason that I know they kept me on the phones. You see, I like to goof around a lot. I have a lot of friends by my desk. They all come over to visit and I stop typing and we all talk. We start laughing and carrying on and I get in trouble. I'm on the phone a lot 'cause a lot of people call me up. I used to get in trouble and then when I was going through the bad time with drugs and everything I was coming in late once in a while. I'm not absent a lot; it's just, like, I have a lot of latenesses. Only by, like, ten to fifteen minutes. See, they're very strict with that. I start at a quarter of eight. If I come in at eight o'clock and if the phones are ringing, they get pissed off. Yeah, you can't blame them. Now, as long as I'm not late and I do my job and I don't do anything outrageous, I can take an hour and a half for lunch; they don't keep time on me. They only watch you when you become suspicious.

I hate the telephones. Sometimes I say, "These friggin' phones!" I hate them because they get you in trouble. Like if the other girl goes somewhere, I can't get up until she comes back. When she's on vacation, it's miserable for me. They make me get a fill-in for my lunch hour and if I don't get one I just stay at my desk. If it wasn't for the phones, that job would be the greatest.

Sometimes I complain because there is nothing, absolutely nothing to get into. I would like a job where I know this job and people will come to me and ask me questions. In other words, these people are just putting papers on my desk for me to type. Do you understand? Just like, there's this guy I know that works in the computers. Now he is so important to them 'cause he knows the computers inside and out. Like, I know my job inside out. They put down a piece of paper; I pick it up; I type it. No thinking. All it takes is the skill of typing.

I asked for a couple of transfers, you know, but it's very hard because I have it so easy where I am that if they have an opening they tell me, "Don't work for him because you'll never get away with what you get away with here." And then it makes me start thinking. And what if I mess myself up? I want to change but then you say, "Well, you know what you got now and it's not bad, but you don't know what you're going to have." And for some jobs they make you management and I say, "Forget it, I don't want it." Because, you see, you have security with the union. Management, if they don't like you, they just tell you to leave, and that's it. When you're part of the union, you get a raise from the contract. When you're part of management your boss gives you your raise so you need to be in good with your boss. The union is pretty good. If you do something like steal from the company, they can't help you but if you're late or something like that, they'll help you or they'll transfer you but they'll keep you in. You won't get fired.

Overall, I think the union is good. We have excellent benefits, but as far as the individual's problems, I think it stinks. Right now I'm doing well on the job and I'm happy there but there was maybe one year ago where I hated it so much that I actually couldn't stop crying. I used to say, "I have to get out of here, I can't take it no more." And sometimes I have been so upset about my job that I have gone over my shop steward. Shop stewards really don't do anything. I have been over his head and I have called the business agent, and they don't do anything either. To me, you got to know somebody if you want to get what you want otherwise you'll just get what everybody else gets.

The girls don't really have to cater to the bosses too much, but there's a great deal going on in the office. It's no Peyton Place but a lot of the bosses, especially the older bosses, do proposition girls. Oh, I could tell you stories, boy! Like, I know some girls—they'll screw around with their boss and everything. But you know, let me tell you something, I know some girl who used to screw around with her boss and he didn't do anything for her. It wasn't even worth her while. But this other girl I know, my very close friend, her boss used to always want to take her to bed and take her out, but she would never go with him. So like, he took good care of her though. Maybe because he was trying to get her, but she never went with him and he took very good care of her. As a matter of fact, he offered to make her management, but once he makes her management, then he's got her. If she's management, her raise depends on him; the other way, she was union. That's how it is.

There are men who have money and they, like, just proposition you. Even union guys, some of them are a little older, they have money, and they just come right out and tell you. Like, one guy showed me a hundred-dollar bill. He'll tell you, "Friday night, you know, I'll take you to dinner, right? Go to a hotel, and then if you want to leave, I'll drop you off." And for a hundred dollars. I never did it. I've borrowed money and paid it back but I never did anything like that. Oh, sometimes they'll come right out directly and tell you what they want but they won't ever threaten you. I guess they could never force you anyway.

I don't think a girl would have to do it because she thinks her job is at stake. But maybe if we weren't in the union and they just picked us at random and we worked for them I'm sure they'd say, "Hey look, I want this, this and that and if you don't do it I'll get rid of you." I'm sure plenty of them would do that.

As far as the future goes, I see none for me. I don't see anything. In other words I have no goals right now. When Tony was around, it was different, but right now I don't see anything. But when my father comes home, I know definitely my life will change. It will be like one big happy family. I don't think he would let me live here.

I really don't know what's going to happen but I think I'll like it, but I guess eventually, like in a year or so, I'll get out of that, too. It won't be new anymore. But that's all I really have to look forward to. What else is there? I want to get a new apartment and I could maybe get a car, but I have no really big images, you know. It does bother me sometimes that if I had married that guy, I would have been married when I was about nineteen and I probably would have had a child when I was about twenty, twenty-one. That would have been dynamite. But you can't have both. Like now, I've had a lot of experience that I would have missed out on. And it was definitely good experience—all that I've been through.

I never realized how sheltered I really was, but when I checked out Manhattan and all those other things, I said, "Wow, this is what's going on out here?" Like, I say to myself, there's so much that my sister doesn't see or know. She only reads about it and hears about it. I still can never get over the poverty, like in Manhattan. Like, I never would believe I would live in an apartment like this. If I didn't go through what I went through, I would never be able to live alone like this. Never. I would never be able to handle all this. I used to cry at the drop of a dime, but now I fight back. Instead of crying, I'll argue. I'll say what I have to say. I got much more bold. I feel that I have to fight for myself because nobody else will. I did definitely get much stronger, and I think that with all I've done and all that happened I really came out all right. Sometimes that amazes me. Especially with the drugs and everything. I believe that somebody is definitely watching me. Sometimes I just say,

"Maybe it's my father." 'Cause a lot of things could have happened—things that my sister would freak out over. Sometimes I think about the things that I've done and I say, "I can't believe it." I really believe somebody likes me; I think about that a lot.

CHAPTER 4

Elinor Thomas

In all the time Michael was sick (with sickle cell anemia), only one thing really hurt my feelings. There's one doctor; she was a fe- male doctor... She made me feel so small... she asked me, "Is Michael your husband's child?"

Elinor Thomas is a small, slim, black woman who is nearly forty. She has an unadorned, straightforward look that is emphasized by dark-rimmed glasses. When she removes her glasses, however, her large, dark eyes dominate her face and her no-nonsense manner is re- placed by a youthful, softer look.

Her husband, John, is a clerk in a New York City post office who earns $13,000 a year. John spends three evenings a week at a local com- munity college studying data processing in the hope that this will help him to advance in his work.

The Thomases have two sons, John Jr., fourteen, and Robert, eight; they had a middle son, Michael, who died of sickle cell disease when he was three years old, and a nephew, Calvin, who lived with them during a good part of their early married life. The family lives in a four-room apartment on the sixth floor of a city-owned housing proj- ect. The clean, well-kept red brick buildings, adjacent to one of many large parks that provide some relief from the concrete and asphalt of the Bronx, are located in a neighborhood which gives one a feeling of relative safety. Their attractively furnished apartment is fastidiously neat and clean although crowded with their belongings. A large color television set dominates the living room, and the tiny kitchen is well equipped. The boys share the larger of two bedrooms, while their par- ents use the smaller one.

The Thomases have been married for eighteen years. They have had severe school problems with their first child and have lost their sec- ond. Now they are worried about the health of their third child. They have raised a nephew and moved from the poverty and danger of one neighborhood to the relative comfort of their present one. Mr. Thomas has worked his way up from a job as a janitor in the post office to his present position as a clerk, and they have struggled endlessly with the question of whether or not Mrs. Thomas, as a good wife and mother, should work.

Elinor talks easily about her life although she is occasionally nervous about her ability to express her own and other people's thoughts and feelings clearly, with appropriate nuance. Threads of what the Chinese call the "bitter past"—her mother's struggle to raise seven children, her husband's childhood and early job experiences—are woven through her description of the present and help to put her perceptions into perspective.

Much of her life seems to be a complex balancing act—shifting a bit to one side, then to the other—in an attempt to satisfy her own, her husband's, and her children's needs, and sometimes those of members of the extended family.

Elinor began by talking about her mother and her own childhood.

Yes, my mother worked. She had to because my father and my mother were separated since I was about six months old, so she went out and did domestic work, and I think she really sacrificed just about her whole life to her children. If she had to scrub her nails off for her children, she would do it to keep her children right. But then when I was about ten or so, she did not work and she began to take care of children for anybody that wanted her to baby-sit.

She—well, she was on welfare for a time; she had to, you know. In those days they used to come out and investigate the home, and a lot of things that you can have on welfare today, we couldn't have. My mother would always have an argument because they couldn't understand why she kept such a beautiful home. My mother's house was immaculate—she was nothing but a perfectionist anyway. And we had everything that was essential—we really had not only the necessities but we had the luxuries, too, because, even though Mother did have a hard time, with the energy and the strength she had she just didn't leave anything out. To me, as far as I can look back on my life, it was important for her to work hard to maintain herself and her family and her home. And then you don't forget on Sunday to go to church to praise God and you thank God for what strength you have and how He made you able to do these things for six days a week.

Altogether there were seven of us, I'm the youngest. And, you know, with me being the youngest, she put an awful lot into me. I took voice lessons, I was in the missionary group, I was in the choir and all these things called for a uniform, a this and a that; there was always a ceremony going on but I always had whatever I needed. I didn't lack anything—I mean material things. I wouldn't do for my kids what my mother did for us or for me. I just can't. And if the other families had steak, we did too. I don't know how. She would walk all the way up to the store and struggle back with two shopping bags. We were the only family that had such things as sliced beets that she would make herself—that stayed in the Frigidaire because this was healthy for you, and there were all kinds of fruit. When my friends wanted a piece of fruit, they came to my house.

Now she lives alone. When I moved here, I thought I would try for a transfer for her, because it was pretty bad where she was living. So she got up here two years after I did. My mother and I, we are close. Sometimes, maybe too close. I don't know how to say this but my sisters and brothers do not look after and call my mother and come to visit her. When she needs and wants someone, Elinor is always the one to go running. I am very reliable to Ma, but it's because I want to be. I feel that she's growing older now and I always admired the type of a woman she was, and I just feel that what I'm doing I want to do. But, you know, when they get older they sort of grow on you, and sometimes—well, I think my mother is a bit too pesty. I'll just tell her, and believe me she'll listen.

She's very proud that we've been married for eighteen years. And I am, other than my older sister, the only child that really has a place to call home, really has a family. I am the only one and the youngest, but yet I am more like a mother figure to my other sister and my brothers, because being the youngest everyone seems to lean on me, you see. And to me it seems it should be the other way around.

Until recently Elinor's nephew, Calvin, has lived with her. She has brought him up from the time he was born and, while she wanted to care for him, she has also felt resentment toward her sister for not being more concerned about her son's welfare and for "dumping" him on her. While the experience with Calvin has clearly been a source of pain as well as pleasure, the extended family was available physically, emotionally, and financially to raise Calvin. Another person in Calvin's mother's position might have been forced to turn to the human-service system for help in some form, such as family day care or foster care, but she was able to rely on her own family. While Calvin obviously has had some problems in dealing with his own identity within the family structure, one cannot doubt that he has benefited enormously from having one surrogate mother who loved him rather than a series of caretakers.

First, I have to say that all along, before he actually came to stay with us, my mother and I used to care for Calvin really more than his mother did. My sister and her husband had been married for about four, five years. They had separated and gone back together, separated and gone back together, and finally the last going back, you know, she became pregnant with Calvin. She was living at home with my mother while her husband was in the service, and he was born there just six months before I got married. And I was just so proud and happy with my little nephew. I was eighteen or nineteen and was working in Bellevue Hospital as a nurse's aide on the evening shift. My sister worked up to two weeks before she had the baby, and when he was three months old she went back to work. That was her thing. No housework, nothing like that. Just working outside, making money. I was so proud of Calvin and I wasn't married, had no children, but I would always help my mother with him. I was always interested in doing things like that.

When I got married, my husband was in the service and her husband was in the service, so my sister and I took this apartment together and the baby stayed at my mother's all week, but on the weekends he was supposed to come home. Well, I would run after work if it was my weekend off and go get the baby from my mother's house. So I wound up being the one to pick up the baby, and when I brought the baby home my sister would just lay in bed on the weekends and sleep. So I took care of the baby and it just became more mine than hers.

Then both of our husbands came home from the service. It got to the point that they weren't getting along—my sister and her husband—and to me, neither one of them had a concern for their child. Her husband was more concerned with her and my sister was just concerned with her job. I used to feel bad about that so I found myself doing even more even though the whole family, and it's a large family, had a share in taking care of him.

What happened was I was working at Bellevue and on my days off I would stop off and pick him up from my mother and take him home. I should have been going out enjoying myself while I didn't have children, but my mind was always on Calvin, doing for Calvin. 'Cause I felt sorry for him, you know, really I did. I loved him. After I became pregnant I left Bellevue and after that, well, I was just lonely. I didn't know what to do with myself and so I would just go down and get him for a week. Then when my first child was eighteen months old my sister came to me and said she was trying it again with her husband and she said, "We would like you to keep Calvin and either his father or I will pick him up on the weekend." So I said, O.K. The reason why she wanted this is because since I was home with my baby, she wanted Calvin to start kindergarten at the school in our neighborhood.

The first few weeks it started out that someone did come to pick him up, but he was very attached to me. He was a very nervous child, too; he would start biting his nails, or he would actually make himself sick because he didn't want to go home. So all right, it worked out a couple of weekends; then finally it was just so bad that they could not live together. They separated again and I don't know what happened to my sister at that point because she just said the hell, she was going to enjoy herself. She had her friends and she did what she wanted to do, and then forget it. She just worked and had a good time and Calvin was actually forgotten.

Well, during that time I had my second child, Michael, and all the time when Michael was younger Calvin was there. I had gotten disgusted with her and we sort of put our foot down. We said, "We're going to send Calvin home on the weekends anyway because you're doing nothing but you're having fun and enjoying yourself. And I can hardly get out." It was one weekend that I called and she didn't answer and I had an aunt that lived in the building where my sister lived so I called Aunt Bertha and I said, "Aunt Bertha, did you see Lucille over the weekend?" So she said, "Yes, I just saw her a few minutes ago coming in the building." So I said, "Oh, well, she thinks she's playing smart with me." So I sent Calvin home.

He was old enough and I had showed, trained, taught him how to go home and it wasn't far from where I lived. I sent him home. He banged, he knocked, he this, he that, he the other, and she didn't answer that door, you know. He went down to my Aunt Bertha's, and of course my Aunt Bertha had the key, you know, like for emergencies or whatever, and anyway when the door was unlocked, my sister was right in the apartment. That hurt me; that hurt her child. So after that, I said, "No. No more." I would not let him face something like this. From that time on Calvin was just here with me and she would come from time to time.

Then Calvin became, what was it, sixteen and he was doing fine. And then my sister, she was talking like the whole world had done her wrong. Everybody was against her and she had started drinking heavy. She had been on her job for ten years and she lost her job by not going to work on Mondays and Tuesdays and that really did something to her. You see, she felt very bad about it, very ashamed toward the family. She would refrain from coming to see anyone in the family and the only one she felt she had to lean on then was her son. And that's when she wanted her son to come home. So, at first, Calvin said, "I'm not going home to my mother." I said, "Well, that's your mother and I have nothing to do with it. She wants you to come home."

But then at the same time, Calvin had started to go to little parties and he was allowed to go, but my husband would make sure he came home at a reasonable time. Then one particular time he went out and he didn't get in until after two o'clock in the morning. I was so nervous with what I thought might have happened that I dozed off but my husband sat up in the bed waiting, and when Calvin came in he didn't give him a good excuse. I think John picked Calvin up and he shoved him. He said, "Get right in your room." And right behind that, I guess Calvin figured, he had another home, he didn't have to stay here. The next thing he was telling his mother on the phone was that he would come home, but she didn't realize what had happened so she was very happy about it.

Now he went home to my sister but he has never lived with his mother; he has never been comfortable living with his mother and things did not change. They got worse, and this is how Calvin began to drop in school. And because my sister, I guess, had felt so guilty, she would not put any kind of curfew, no type of restrictions on him. I remember once I called down there and I wanted to speak to him and it was ten-thirty at night. He was still sixteen. And she said, "Calvin has just left to go to the movies." Well, I almost went through the phone. I got so upset because I figured that all my years and all that I thought I was doing is all going down the drain.

So this is what actually happened. Calvin went in the service. He left his mother, conned her into signing him up, and he went into the navy, but he didn't like it. So he stayed one year, then he got out in June. Now on Monday, no, yesterday, Calvin met me at Robert's school. I was standing there waiting when I saw someone walk up. He said, "What's the matter, you don't recognize your own child?" I said, "Oh, Calvin."

It's just sad. Calvin, to me, Calvin wants to come back, but he's too much of a man to come and ask. He had a job and he said he got laid off. He is supposedly in night school now, making up his last year of school. My husband had a good talk with him. He let him know, "Calvin, I know what you're doing, you know. You'll mess yourself up for life." I still feel bad and sad about it, but there's nothing I can do. I think now it's too late. And sometimes I even feel, when he comes to the school to meet me, he comes up to me like he looks up to me. And it hurts. I don't know why it should hurt me. I feel good about it, but it hurts to see how he, how he treats his mother, in a sense. I guess it has to come out on somebody though.

Ever since she became pregnant with her first child, Elinor's employment outside the home has been a source of conflict between herself and her husband. She has derived enormous gratification from working as a nurse's aide in a hospital, and for many years she wanted to return to work but, while they could use the extra money, her working has conflicted acutely with her husband's image of her as a wife and mother and, to some extent, it has conflicted with her own views of her responsibilities.

You know, I feel that when I worked at Bellevue maybe I was too young to work in a psychiatric hospital. How I got to Bellevue was after I graduated from high school I was working in a factory for a while but then someone said to me, "Why don't you come down to Bellevue because they're hiring now?" So I went down and I had an interview. After I was accepted and had my physical, they sent me a card to go to a psychiatric training class for a month and that's how I got in. I must have been eighteen or nineteen.

I got married while I was working there and when I had little John four years later that's when I left. I finally went in to resign 'cause my husband did not want me to go back to work once I had the baby. In my mind I had thought my mother would take care of my baby and I would go back, but I think I was a little too young to be working in a psychiatric hospital. I wasn't very objective; I used to worry so much about the patients, and when things happened it really would tear me apart. I would just keep myself worked up and upset, and he never felt it was the right place for me to work—in psycho— and once I had his baby he felt he didn't need any other interference, like when I came home and would be upset. I really did enjoy my work and I was very angry with my husband because he did not want me to go back, but I was very proud of my first baby so I realized that I wasn't going against his word.

After John Jr. was born I went out a little per diem, but actually it was eleven years before I had a regular job. Then I said to my husband before we moved here, "Now the kids are big enough." Robert wasn't, but I feel in a way that I was running from something else, too. I felt that even though Robert was a baby, with what I had gone through with Michael, I had to pull myself away a bit from my family and my husband. But I think he was feeling the other way, you know, like, "No, no, he needs you. You stay home." But he didn't put his foot down. He said, "If you want to work, Elinor, and want to go back into the hospital, go ahead but change your shift." He didn't like my not being home on the weekend. He feels the whole family should be home on the weekend together.

I went back, and they put me into pediatrics and I loved it. I had to go to class again because it had been eleven years, so after the classes the teacher called me inside and she says to me, "You made out very well in class." And she says, "I know about your misfortunes and what not, and we would like to know if you think you could work in 'Peds' 'cause that's a special ward. We got your reference from Bellevue. You got a beautiful record, and after working there for six years we don't seem to understand why you didn't even try to go into an L.P.N.* school." So I explained to her that even though now I feel that that might be one of my desires, that Robert was only two and that I was still a little nervous and edgy about his condition, and I told her I would prefer waiting until he got older before I attempt to go into any kind of school because I knew that if anything happened to my kids I would just stop. I would give up.

But I accepted going into Peds, and that sort of upset my husband because even though he is dedicated to his job he feels that I am (laughs), that I am dedicated even more. You know, I love my kids but when I was working at the hospital if it was time for me to get off at three-thirty and there was an emergency and I'm walking out off the ward and the doctor's hollering for something, I would turn back. It was things like that. Then when we started having problems with little John in school, he had a good excuse—a good reason for saying, "Leave the job." And of course in the back of his mind, too, was that he felt that I was neglecting Robert. But he is a person who feels that a woman's place is in the home to take care of the children, her own children. Then I had begun to feel a little guilty because John wasn't doing well in school and I says, "You know, I had better stop before something happens and then I would be more or less to blame for it." So that's when I stopped.

I worked fourteen months. When I stopped I felt a bit bitter. I was very angry. For a while it was like I was blaming everybody in the household for my having to stop working. Even

* Licensed Practical Nurse.

little John. Sometimes even after I stopped I was still being called to school. And I would go to talk to the teachers and I would walk the four blocks home with tears in my eyes. And then by the time in the evening when my husband came home I was just (*laughs*) mad, you know. And he might have said one or two words to me and I says, "Well, I've stopped working and the same thing is going on." I just felt that I was being pulled away from something that I enjoyed doing for another problem and it didn't help. Now I think that the anger has gone away and so I'm just resigned about staying home, just being in the household until Robert is maybe ten or twelve.

When I was working, I was bringing in something like a hundred and sixty dollars every two weeks and, you know, you feel so good to be able to do a lot of things that we could not do before. And I wasn't being selfish; it wasn't like *my* money. It was to be shared by everyone. Back when I started working I said to my husband, "Let's make it like once every two weeks we eat out." I was actually trying to please him because he really enjoys eating out and the children enjoyed it. We used to take the kids downtown to different shows and I felt good because I said, "This is like an extra salary and now we can do this." I also feel that my husband—how should I say it—he wants to be needed, he wants to be the top one in the household, and maybe he didn't feel that way when I was working.

The problem was I was too afraid because we were having problems with little John, and with my being out of the house I just, I had a fear that if anything happened that my husband might have blamed me for it, and I had to be more careful and think about that because of the loss of Michael. I think my husband reacted much more than I did. I was able to get over it in a sense, but with him, even with the baby now, Robert, he's— there's something there, you know. His loss of Michael and the feeling that Robert might have some part of that sickness. He's very, very close to Robert, and he still feels that he has the fear of something happening to him.

But sometimes I feel like I have a mind of my own and I should be able to do, you know, exactly what I want because I feel that I'm not a person that goes to extremes. But now I don't feel too bad about it because I always look forward to one day—the kids are growing up. I can see it now with John—he's going to be fourteen next week and I see he's growing up. So now there's only Robert.

I asked Elinor how she viewed herself and her family economically.

I feel, and I also feel that my husband feels, that he is more or less in the middle-income bracket. I hope I'm saying this right, because I get nervous sometimes. I feel that he feels like he's going to school, he's trying to further himself in a way, but yet he has that feeling that he's not going to go up so much higher. Do you understand? And I feel, compared with what he had earned before, there is such a great difference from then to now that—whenever you can go and have charge accounts and whenever you can eat halfway decent and get the things you want and be comfortable then you do consider yourself more in the middle-income bracket. Even though most of the time it always means big, big sacrifice.

My mother always said to me, "Elinor, you are a very fortunate girl—to be married just eighteen years and have everything that you want or need in your home, and all you have to do is open your mouth and you've got it." And when she says this she's thinking of how hard it was in her time just to struggle and put clothes on your children and feed them halfway decent, and it took many, many, many years for her to have what I've got in such a small space of time. And I can see that.

I can show you another example with my mother. My mother will go out and buy shoes and stock the closet with shoes or dresses. "Ma, why are you buying another pair of shoes? You just bought a pair last month." She says, "Whether I wear them or whether I never put them on my feet, I can remember the day when I had to patch up my shoes to get out to go to work just for my family to survive." And she feels so good about the fact that she has come over that water now, that she just feels that whatever she wants to do, however she wants to fix her home, she doesn't want anyone to stop her or to say anything.

My husband and I do feel, especially now, that we're in a middle-income bracket, and maybe it has a lot to do with the way your children are raised, too. How should I say? My children have never actually lived in what you call the ghetto. My children have never actually had to go through a lot of things that I see—shacky houses with the ceiling hanging down, no water, no heat, this type of thing.

I could actually say that since my mother moved from Harlem when I was five years old—I don't remember anything about Harlem or the type of apartment she lived in—I've never had that type of thing. The tenements, they're old, but they were well kept. Now if I go back to the neighborhood where I grew up, it brings tears sometimes. I don't have a whole lot of money and maybe when all is done, around a pay period or at the end of the month, you might not have that much left, but everything that I want is in my home. Anything that might break down in my home, I am able to have fixed. I would have it—with health or strength—I would have it no other way. The only way I would go down is maybe if, God forbid, like I lost my husband and financially I really went in a hole, and I don't think I would go that far down then. I just don't think I would.

But you always have a feeling that you're not going to be able to earn but so much, you know. I think this is a feeling in a lot of black people's minds, especially the head of the family, even my husband. In the post office my husband took a test one time for a foreman or something like that. He passed it, so I thought he was going to take the job, but he said he just wanted to know if he was able to pass that test.

Then he took a test for supervisor. He missed it by some points. He took that test again. That test was even less. He took it for the third time; it was even less and he just had this funny feeling. He says, "It's impossible." He studied more and he knew more with almost the same test. He went down, down, down. He couldn't understand it. He knew a particular person that took the same test and had failed it. But that person got the position, you see. And quite naturally you know that did not make him feel good at all, because he knew the person failed the same test. Yes, this person was white; it was a woman. I

couldn't understand it. Well, he explained it to me and I lis-
tened. He said, "You're not going to get but so high. Some
people do but you've got to be, excuse my expression, damn
good if you get there. And then when you get there, if you're
black, you've got to shine." This is the way he feels. At first he
was very angry about it, but I think that the majority of black
folk are just beginning to accept it. The majority—I guess I
shouldn't have said that—I should say my husband has sort of
accepted the fact that he's going to live a life and he's going to
live it as good and do as much as he can in the ways that he can,
and that's it.

I manage the money. When my husband gets paid he
cashes his check and he deposits some right then and there, and
then he comes home and he puts his salary down on the dresser
and that way I know how to work. I blow my top when I go to
the store and see the prices going high, high, and then I make
up my mind, am I going to buy it or am I not going to buy it? But
then somehow or another, I find that the things we are used to
eating, we still eat. The steak is not the better cut, but I really
haven't cut out anything really.

The rent—to me, it's reasonable. We pay a hundred and
thirty-one dollars for these four rooms, and there was just an increase the first of July. The year before it was a hundred and
twenty-one dollars, and your lights and your gas—everything is
included. I'm very pleased because the neighborhood is not a
bad neighborhood. But even if I had to pay more to be in a sort
of decent neighborhood, I would. I'm not one to be out too often at night, anyway. I have to go to some meetings, but I try to
get in at a certain time. Or I try to take a cab. I won't be walking
those dark streets. And there are some times that I take little
John along with me. I'm a very nervous person so I always have
a fear of something happening. Because I've lived in public
housing so long, I know a lot of things can go on, and I just have
a fear of elevators. And every day of my life, when I push that
door, I'm always looking, you know. It's on my mind. But, it's
pretty decent.

I would love to be in my own place, a home, a house of my
own, but it's not easy. And as far as my husband is concerned,

he feels that it is too late for a house, but he would maybe love to move out of the city to a garden apartment or something like that. Maybe one day . . .

Sickle cell anemia is an inherited blood disorder caused by an alteration in hemoglobin. The disease, which is found in Africa and in Mediterranean countries, now afflicts over six hundred thousand blacks in the United States. Two-and-a-half million Americans—one in ten— carry the sickle cell trait, caused by a single abnormal gene. If a child receives an imperfect gene from both parents he or she acquires the disease. On the average, one in four children of parents with the trait will have the disease and an additional two out of four will carry the trait into the next generation. There is no known cure.

Michael was two and a half when he got sick. He had started running a fever, and when I took him up to the hospital they took an X ray and they couldn't find anything wrong with him. So I just brought him back home and then the fever was really getting high and then they did another X ray on him and they found that he had a small patch of pneumonia.

So then in those days, knowing he had pneumonia, you had to run back every single day for him to get an injection. And getting him dressed one morning I myself noticed that his hands and his fingers were all swollen. And if I would touch the area, he would cry. So when I got him up there that morning this one doctor says, "Why are his hands swollen, Mother?" I said, "I don't know." So they said, "We have to take a blood test on him." So they drew the blood and they sent it up and I had to wait there just about the whole day for the results. And they called me and they asked me did I know what sickle cell was. That's how they found out.

So then they asked all of us in the family to come in and have the tests. They found at first that my husband did not have the trait, little John had nothing, and I was a sickle cell trait. I was a sickle cell trait—which I never knew in my life. By the time they explained to me what the sickness was all about and how it happens and the crisis and what not, I found that even though the pneumonia had cleared in a week or two, in less than a month the first crisis came on and he was in the hospital. And then it just kept going. But actually it only lasted about sixteen months. I found out when he was exactly two and a half and he died two months before his fourth birthday.

In all the time Michael was sick, only one thing really hurt my feelings. There's one doctor; she was a female doctor. Michael was upstairs in the hospital on the ward and I had to go down to the hematology clinic to get the results of our blood tests, and that particular doctor, she really hurt my feelings very bad. She made me feel less than a—than anything. She made me feel so small. She said it's impossible for Michael to have sickle cell disease and I'm a trait and my husband is not a trait. So, I says, "Well, that's it." So she asked me, "Is Michael your husband's child?" And I mean she really hurt me, you know. I jumped back, like that, and I got hot all over. I says, "Of course he is." And I says, "But that is my only—that's my husband, you know!" I mean like she really embarrassed me; she made me feel so bad.

Now it's all right to ask some questions, to ask somebody a question like that, but then she gets up from her desk and she walks around and she closes the door and she says to me, "Come on, you can tell me the truth. I will never mention it and I won't put it down on the records." I said, "I told you the truth." And at that minute tears started coming out of my eyes. So she still insisted that it was impossible. But then the thing that really got to me is that I told her when I first went into her office that Michael was upstairs and he's going through his first crisis, and my husband was upstairs with him, so she says to me, "Well, when you go upstairs you don't have to mention it to your husband."

When I took that elevator and went upstairs, I was overflowing on the inside. I was burning up hot. And the moment I walked on to the ward and saw my husband, I broke out crying and I just ran and fell in his arms. And he got all upset. He said, "What happened, what happened?" And I just cried and I told my husband, "She is trying to tell me that you're not Michael's father." And then I had to turn around and get myself together and plead 'cause he was ready to go downstairs and blast, you know, all over. Of all the things that happened I think that's the worst part of it.

When Robert was born, they tested him, and he didn't have sickle cell and I was so happy about that. But then a year later they tested him again and they found out. So the doctor sort of explained to me that they did a different type of a test that was more extensive on the family and that's when they found that my husband had a thalassemia trait, another form of anemia, so now when it comes to Robert, he's sickle thalassemia, that's what he has. But he is at much less risk. He should not go through these crises and what not. And thank God, I've had no real deep problems with him. You know, every once in a while he had a little patch of pneumonia that kind of shook me. When he had that little mild asthma attack, that kind of shook me. But he's never gone through a crisis. So far.

At the time of his death Michael had pneumonia. But that last time he ran a fever again, I took him up to the hospital and my husband, he stayed home from work and he went with me because Michael couldn't walk. When we got up to the hospital we saw one of the doctors that knew him from the ward and he examined him all over and, well, he didn't send Michael up to have an X ray taken and I guess, sometimes you're so upset about your children being sick, I didn't even think to mention it to him. He said, "Well, Mother, even though he has a fever, it has to be something, but I can't find anything wrong with him and he's been in the hospital so much. Take him back home and if the fever doesn't come down, then bring him back." And actually he had pneumonia all the time.

I would not blame—it's a funny thing—when I think of it I try to get my mind off of it fast, you know, because I say, like, a little neglect on maybe the doctor's part, knowing that he was a sickle cell patient, and sometimes I feel a little bit bad but not enough to say that I blame it on myself because I said if only I had mentioned it . . . Then I try to think this way—that the doctor's not to fault and, Mommy, you're not to fault because it was God's will. And it just happened the way it was supposed to happen.

I brought Michael home the last time, I think it was a Friday. Over the weekend I got the fever down and on that Monday he was just so happy and full of smiles and I had to go to the clinic because I was seven months pregnant. And my husband, it's the funniest thing, my husband had to work every other weekend then and he would always get Wednesday and Thursday off. This particular time he had a Monday off. That was right before Easter, and my mother had given me money to buy the kids jelly beans, so I went to the clinic and I felt so relaxed because I didn't have to worry about rushing home.

Then when I came home, my husband says, "You know, Michael has been sleeping with me almost all day long." So I said, "Well, now that I'm home, bring him in the living room and just see if he'll sit up." And I started my dinner. I felt him and he was not warm. I would have taken his temperature, but he always gets burning up hot in his hand and he wasn't warm. But I sent Calvin down to get a bottle of Coca Cola and ginger ale. He bought it and came back upstairs, and my husband poured some ginger ale and he was trying to give it to Michael with a straw. And I was cooking and all of a sudden I heard him say, "Michael!" I dropped everything and I ran to the door and I saw him turning—and he was just—and I said, "Oh Lord, my child!" And I ran to him and I ran away. And my husband said, "He's all right, he's all right." And right away, I don't know why, I says, "Don't tell me that. Something has gone wrong." So I ran to the phone and I started crying and I called my older sister who is a nurse and my sister said, "Get him to the hospital quick." So then my husband laid him down, and you know how the eyes, his eyes got real starry and glassy, and I said, "Michael, Michael?" And he said, "Hh-m-m." That's all he would say to me. (Her voice breaks.) Then he, you know, he made a b.m. and I said, "Oh, my Lord." I called my neighbor upstairs and I asked could I send the kids up to her, because we had to rush Michael to the hospital. So she ran downstairs to my apartment and she grabbed him, and I started screaming and I ran to my drawer, you know, to get money out, 'cause I knew we had to take a cab, and as I ran my husband just grabbed the blanket out of the closet and he said, "Come on, Elinor, we have to go." And I ran out in the hall screaming. My husband grabbed him just the way he was and ran, and I ran.

I'm screaming in the street and couldn't find no cab and I'm still screaming *(voice breaking)*. And my husband saw the patrol car and he flagged it down. He ran with the baby and I'm running behind him and the patrol car stopped and I says, "Take my child to the hospital—he has sickle cell." So they put on their lights and their sirens and then they told my husband, "Keep breathing in his mouth, Father." And my husband kept breathing and I'm still screaming and crying. *(Crying openly now.)* And as we went up the street I saw a station wagon coming. *(Pause. Deep breath.)* I can't explain how people say they see death, but to me, it's like I saw death. Like I just saw myself in heaven, all of us. This car never stopped and the police car— bang, right into it—and it was just a terrible thing.

So then all of a sudden I see the streets were black with people and I'm still screaming, "My baby! My baby!" And they got another patrol car there right away. And when I stepped out of the first car, that's when they noticed that I was expecting. So then they rushed us to a closer hospital and as soon as we got there, the cops, everybody, jumped out of the car and my husband got out and the cop grabbed Michael out of his hands and all the nurses and doctors were outside waiting for this emergency. And I ran through and I started screaming and I said, "He's got sickle cell," 'cause I always remember someone saying if anything happens make sure you say what he has. And I ran and I was saying, "John, call my mother, call your mother. John, call somebody." And he went to call them, and the cop, the policeman, came out and as soon as the policeman came out, he said, "Where's your husband?" 'cause I was hysterical like, you know. I said, "He went to call my mother."

So then, well, somebody went and got him out of the phone booth. And when they went and got him out of the phone booth I said, "I know." I knew that he was gone. So then they put us in a room, and my husband had to give them all the information. And then they said the doctor will be coming. So the doctor came. She said to me, "Do you have any more children at home?" I said, "Yes, I have a son. But is my son gone? Is he dead? I know he's dead, you know." She nodded. I said, "I want to see him." So then the cops and the nurse, the doctors and all, they said no. I said, "I want to see my child. You can't tell me I can't see my child." He was in the blanket and I just kissed him and hugged him, but he was gone. *(Elinor removes her glasses, wipes away her tears, and puts the glasses on the table.)* So then they offered to call a cab for us, and when we got in the cab then my husband got upset. And it's funny how we are. When he gets upset, I calm down. He just broke down. The first time in my life I heard a man cry the way he did. Then we got home and the girl from upstairs, she said, "Where's Michael? They kept him?" And I just said, "My son is gone."

He was buried on Good Friday. It was my idea that I wanted him laid out in a white suit and white shoes; I just wanted him laid out in white. And on Easter Sunday my husband, all day he cried and cried and cried and cried. So I tried to brace myself together. And then I got over it, you know.

And this is when little John started failing in school. You know, when he started out he was doing well. When he failed, or when he started his daydreaming was after my son passed. After that he just stopped and he would just sit and stare out the window. I have some feeling—I wonder if John thought that he was, you know, the cause of Michael's death, but then I think again, and say to myself that he has no reason to feel this way. I just don't know. Even now, it might be a period like for a week or so, John does nothing in school. And all of a sudden, maybe the next week, for two, three days, he works beautifully.

And Robert, when he was born, looked just like Michael. And he used to talk like him. Everybody said it. And even John Jr. at one time was very frightened and fearful of Robert because he looked just like Michael.

Through the years little John has become very close with me, and Robert has become very close with his father. I think it's because John's worried about Robert, worried about something happening to him. I feel that once you've had something hard hit you like that, nothing else can hurt you half as bad. God, I hope that we will always have Robert, but I think that if he passed away, I would not be as hurt as I was the first time. The first time was like a shock to me, you know. I just felt so bad about it. I thought everybody, not everybody, but I just felt God was so unfair, so unjust. I used to say, "Why God, why?" And it's like saying he gave me my answer, and then I realized: I have Robert, I have John; but in the beginning I couldn't see it this way.

I don't worry half so much now about Robert, but my husband's got such strong feelings. I don't like to hear him saying he feels that something is going to happen, and I find myself telling him to pray to God and ask God to take that feeling away from him and just live comfortably with Robert, because we're all going, we're leaving one day. I find myself talking more than necessary and fast with my husband when he feels this way, and when he expresses himself to me I don't want to hear. I really don't want him to think it, you see. Like his thinking and thinking as strongly as he does is like saying it really will happen.

I'm not much up on women's lib, you know, but I don't think I would want to be equal with my husband or with a man completely. I just feel that the man is the stronger sex and I think it's nice when you can look up to the man as your husband. I mean, he's supposed to be the biggest thing in the household, you know.

I asked Elinor if she didn't feel that in many ways she was just as strong as her husband.

In actuality I feel I am. I feel, to be truthful, that I'm keeping myself down, that I am the strongest one. In a sense I feel my husband looks up to me, but somehow or another, I try to tone that down and make him stay up there because I feel that's the way it should be. My husband is very, very firm, knows what he wants and how he wants to go about it, but when he was growing up, his mother always felt that he could not do this, that, and the other as well as his older brother. Yet when we got married, I put it together in my mind, and from what I saw of my husband, I found that he could do it, but he always had the feeling that he could not. My husband still is a very doubtful person, doubtful of himself. I feel that since we were married, I have brought out a lot of things with my husband that maybe might have surprised him, that he didn't know he was capable of doing. I want him to feel that he is important. I think he does, too.

I might be putting myself down, but I always have faith and hope that one day I'll go back to school or go back to nursing and, well, if that day doesn't come, so it doesn't come. I feel that day might come by the time little John is all well adjusted and is doing much better in school, and when Robert grows up to be a little older, too. You know, all these things I feel are important. I have a whole lot of feelings. I feel that my husband is a good man. He's a good husband, a good father, and he's still pushing, still trying, and I might even feel one day that we'll be happier in a sense when maybe all my little dreams and the many things that together we have wished for might come true. And I'm willing to wait and take the chance and see.

I was really wondering, how am I going to talk on women's lib? But I guess you really have to think of yourself and then—I do feel that my kids feel very happy, very comfortable, very warm, because they always can push the door and there's Ma, you know. And I do know how my husband feels. I can even notice that some nights he gets a little tired when he's out late at school. I have a warming tray, so after dinner I set it up and I put my husband's food on this tray and plug it in there. Sometimes I'm so tired after the kids are in bed that I might lay down for a little while and I forget to set the alarm. And I can sense the difference even in that. I can sense that my husband feels happier when he comes in and I'm up—even though he knows that I'm tired. One or two of my friends, they say, "You're nuts." But I think a whole lot of things are important and people, sometimes, this women's lib and the way the world is going, they seem to forget so much. I know my husband likes me to be up, and maybe tonight I might light a candle, make a nice little setting, make everything warm, and, who knows, I might even throw on something, you know, look a little different. And in his way, he does the same. I don't have to do it, but I really want to do it, straight from my heart.

Since these conversations, Elinor Thomas has decided to take in a foster child rather than work outside her home. A handsome little boy has been living with them for some time and has become a member of the family. She knows that this decision will postpone her return to hospital work, but she thinks that it is the right decision for the entire family. She says, "I feel like I could be a lot of help to a child, and the child will be a lot of help to me. 'Cause I guess—I don't know—how should I say it? Well, I feel I am the motherly type but you can become very lonely as your kids grow up and move away from home. I might as well have another baby to mother..."

CHAPTER 5

Maria Perez

I am neither a heroine nor a victim.

Maria Perez is a small, slim, woman in her late thirties who came to this country from Latin America when she was twenty-one. Her face is angular with pronounced cheekbones and large dark eyes; she wears her long dark hair in a page boy that flips up at the front. When we first met she was wearing red pants and a white peasant blouse with blue and red embroidery on the front, back, and sleeves. She was meticulously dressed each time we talked even though she had just come from work.

Maria expressed considerable anxiety about what I was writing and was concerned that her privacy would be disturbed. Although I reassured her repeatedly that whatever she told me was confidential and that names would be changed, she nevertheless remained very anxious. She preferred to "talk in the street or in a park where you have more privacy," so we sat and talked on a park bench adjacent to an elevated train track. When trains roared by every few minutes making it impossible to talk or to hear, we simply waited until they had passed and then continued. Maria speaks nearly perfect English with only a slight Spanish accent. Occasionally she searches for the exact word she wants but, while she disparages her ability to speak English, she is actually fluent.

She works in the mornings as a floor secretary on the cancer floor of a large teaching hospital. The hospital is within a few blocks of her home and near the day care center attended by her two younger children. Her husband is a commercial artist in the catalogue department of a large department store. The oldest of their three children, a boy, is six-and-a-half years old. He has just completed the first grade. The second child, a girl, is five years old, and the youngest is a boy of four. I was referred to Maria by the director of the day care center that her younger children attended at the time we first talked.

She began by talking about her children.

93

My four-year-old is not really happy at the Center. He has never quite gotten used to it. I don't know why not. He is not the happy baby that my other children were. Perhaps it is because my life was not going the way I wanted it to when he was a baby. He gets angry and fights with the other children. My oldest boy did very well in the first grade. He goes to a parochial school because I didn't want to send him to public school. The other two children will stay in the Center until they're ready to go to first grade because they don't have a kindergarten at the parochial school.

I had another child, too, a little girl. She died. I would have had two boys and two girls—four children. She died when she was one year old. She had ear infections and then a high fever and went into the hospital one day and died the next. Three or four days before, I brought her to the doctor and told him that she wasn't well and that she wasn't eating, and he said, "Oh, that's all right, just give her rice and beans." He gave her some injections and sent us home. Maybe he could have done something for her then.

It was such a shock when she died because she was just about one year old and you know how you celebrate all the things they learn during that first year. But my sister was even more upset when my little girl died than I was, and although I was all broken up inside I had to comfort her. I told her that I was pregnant again and that that baby would be a boy; my sister always liked little boys. I told her that it was God's will that my little girl died and that it would be all right when I had the new baby. I do feel as though it was God's will. I believe very much in God and I feel that what happens is what He has done.

After she died I used to go to visit her at the cemetery all the time—I used to go every Sunday, even when I was pregnant—but I realized that it wasn't doing her any good; it wasn't doing me any good. I was just very upset. So I stopped going to the cemetery altogether until after I had the baby and after I got a hold of myself. Then later when I felt better, I started going again every now and then. I would bring flowers and put them on her grave. I've told the children that they have a sister—my little girl says that she has a sister but she's in heaven. Now they come with me to visit the cemetery and to put flowers on her grave.

Some people told me that I should have sued the doctor, but I didn't want to do that. What difference does money make? What would I have gained? Fifteen or twenty thousand dollars? What difference does it make? *(She shrugs her shoulders.)* Money doesn't mean that much to me. Money is part of life, but I didn't want to do that. I didn't even agree to have an autopsy because I was feeling so bad. I watched her suffer so much that day in the hospital that I didn't want it done. And they wouldn't have told me the truth about why she died anyway.

I work as a secretary in a hospital on the cancer floor. At first it was very hard work because I wasn't used to working with patients. I got very upset because the patients were so sick and because so many of them died. But gradually I learned that I had to separate myself from them, not get to know them very well, not be very friendly with them, so that it wouldn't affect me so much when they died.

I've never worked with patients before, but it was a very good job for me because it's part-time and because it's so close to the Center where my children go. At first I thought about working full-time downtown, but that would have meant my leaving my children at seven in the morning and not getting back until six or seven in the evening, and that's just too much. This is just right. And I've learned a lot from working at this job. I've learned to feel compassion for people and I've learned what's important in life. I've learned that whether you have steak today and don't have it tomorrow isn't that important, but that it is really your health that's the most important thing.

I came to this country when I was twenty-one. I had graduated from high school in Ecuador and had my diploma in literature and philosophy. After I finished school I worked for a nun who had an English-Spanish academy. Then she came to this country and after she was here about a year she suggested that I might want to come here too, and so she helped me. I never would have been able to get here if it hadn't been for her. She gave me a helping hand.

When I got here I didn't speak any English. I got here on a Thursday and by the next Monday morning I was working in a factory downtown, sewing by hand. I didn't use the machine because I didn't know how to. I worked there for six months but I left because everybody in the factory spoke Spanish so I couldn't learn any English that way. Then I went to work for Horn and Hardart—you remember Horn and Hardart? I worked as a—how do you say it—I picked up the dishes on the tables— a bus girl—that's it. It was a terrible job. The people there spoke English so that I could start learning English, but it was a very hard job. As I was picking up the dishes from the tables the tears were streaming down my face because in my country only people of the lower class do that kind of work and I had the idea in my head that everybody was looking at me saying, "Look at what kind of work she is doing."

After a while they put me behind the counter and that was very hard also. I had to serve people behind the counter and I didn't know very much English, and sometimes I used to hide behind there so that people wouldn't ask me anything. The other people I worked with, a Greek couple, said, "If you don't speak English you should get out of here." But one woman, a German woman, told me that this was this and that was that and helped me to learn.

But it was very hard, and sometimes I did not know whether I could stay in this country. I had not yet paid for my ticket here and I was thinking about going back because I was crying all the time and I didn't think that I could survive. One day I went into a church and I stayed there a whole hour. I was all by myself, I saw nobody else there, and I cried and talked to God for that whole hour. (Mrs. Perez struggles not to cry.) I said to God, "If it's the best thing for me to stay then give me the strength to stay here, and if it isn't, then let me go back to my country." (Her eyes fill with tears and she is barely in control.) When I left that church I was a different person—I felt I had the strength to go on. I came out happy and singing.

Soon after that I said to myself that I cannot do that work anymore—that is not the kind of work for me. I have to work in an office. So I went to night school and I learned typing and then I got a job in a taxi company. The bookkeeper there taught me a lot. She really helped me and I worked there for five years. Then I got a better job downtown making more money, but after I worked there for two years I got pregnant and I had to leave.

I had planned that I wouldn't go back to work until my youngest child went into the first grade, but I couldn't go along with that plan because things did not go the way that I had intended. I decided about two-and-a-half years ago that I had to go to work if we were to survive, and so I went to get some training. But you know, I had not worked for several years. If you put that down on a job application and somebody else worked a month ago you know they're going to take the other person, so I decided I better get some training.

I went to Manpower and studied speedwriting and I brushed up on my typing. Also my English was not so good because I have lived with my family where we spoke only Spanish. When I first went to Manpower I was very surprised at the people who were also taking courses there. They were all lower class; they were poor; they were on welfare. I had been living in the shell of my family and had not realized what life was like outside. The language that people used! Some of them would not go out of their houses without a weapon! I was so shocked. I hadn't realized that people lived like this and I nearly quit the training program, but I decided that I had begun and I had to finish. I like challenges. I like every little new thing that I learn and I like to set up challenges for myself, so I was determined to finish. After I finished I applied to work in the hospital about ten times. I worked very hard at getting this job because it was just the right place for me to work.

I grew up in the highlands of Ecuador about an hour outside of the capitol, Quito. My father had a big house, lots of land in the countryside, and had people working for him to take care of the land. My grandmother also had a house farther out in the countryside; she had chickens, sheep, and a cow or two, and she also had people taking care of her land. We sometimes went to visit my grandmother but my father was very strict and would not even let us go there very often. But my mother was more lenient. My father was a salesman and had a very good business so when he was away from home my mother would let us go places. But then my father's business began to fail. First we had to sell one house, and then things got very bad for him. We moved to the city when I was fifteen or sixteen, but I had lived in the country for so long that I loved the country.

That was one of the reasons that I decided to come to this country—my father's business was so bad that I wanted to help him. I wanted to help him make things go better. My father was so strict I don't know how he ever let me come to this country. I think maybe it was partly because the woman who suggested that I come here, my friend who ran the academy, was a nun and he felt that anybody who was a nun would be O.K. for me to be with.

After I finished high school in Ecuador I wanted to go to the university but you had to pay, and we did not have enough money so I had to give it up. That's another reason I wanted to come here—so that I could further my education.

And I wanted to bring my brothers and sisters over too. First I brought a brother and sister, and together we worked to bring the rest of the family. Why me? I don't know. I have always wanted to do things for other people and to take care of other people. It is my pleasure. My sister tells me now that, even when I was a little girl, I would say, "When I am grown up I will take care of all of you." The first few months when I was in this country and I was working in that factory I was only making about thirty-five dollars a week, but around Mother's Day I took ten dollars out of my thirty-five dollars and I sent it to my mother and it gave me such a wonderful feeling, such pleasure to send that ten dollars to my mother for Mother's Day.

First my brother and sister came over. My older sister—she still lives in Ecuador. She's married and has four children but, you know, everything in life does not go just right. Her husband is a son of a gun. He runs around with another woman and my sister is not too happy, but it's too late for her to come over because I don't want to take the responsibility of four children and of breaking up a home. But my younger brother and sister came over and we worked together to bring over another younger brother who came to school here. Later, another sister came and we all worked together to bring over my parents, and finally my youngest three brothers came over just about five years ago.

I wanted them all to finish their education and to make something of themselves, and they have. Some of my brothers finished high school here in this country, and they all speak English. One of my sisters had to stop her studies because she got headaches when she studied so she works as a key-punch operator. My big brother is married and has two children, and he's an auto mechanic. My other brother is a supervisor in a large company, and I have another brother who's finishing up at a local community college. He's going to be a bilingual teacher. My younger sister who's finishing up next year—she will be a nurse. Another brother is finishing at City College—he's going to be an engineer. And my youngest brother is finishing his degree in chemistry and wants to go on to study medicine. It's funny—all of my brothers and sisters are getting their education, and I came over in order to get more of an education and I'm over thirty and still do not have a diploma. But I am going to school too, part-time, and I want to get a diploma. I went to night school before I had the children, and now I have been going as a matriculating student since last year. I go in the morning and have about ten credits so far, but I'm not too old to get my degree. I want to take psychology or social work or something and help people.

My family all live in one house together. My brother and sister-in-law and his two children live on the bottom floor; we live on the middle floor with my three children; my parents and my five brothers and two sisters live together up on the top floor. We bought the house because if we each paid rent it would cost much more money. We all get along very well—no problems. When one is sad we try to cheer him up and when one is happy we all share in the happiness. And on holidays, Christmas, and so forth, we all get together and have a good time. They are all making their own path in life and they are all making something of themselves.

I have one sister, the one who is a key-punch operator, she's going with a fellow now. At first my father was very upset because he's not Catholic—he's Jewish—but now he feels all right about it. And another sister of mine is going with an Italian boy. But you know in this country you have to be very careful whom you go with, and you have to take your time.

We have such a big family and we're used to living together; that's why I was so sad when I was first in this country. I didn't know the language and I didn't know the customs and it was hard being alone without my family around me. But I left it all up to God. I wanted to bring them over and I wanted to do something for them but I said to God, "If it's going to be good for them, then you make it all easy for me and if it isn't going to be good for them then make it so hard that I won't be able to do it." And then I put a blindfold on my eyes and worked, and it was so easy. First I brought over two, then two more, then my parents, then the last three, but all with God's and each other's help.

When we met for the second time Maria told me about how she had obtained a place for her children in the day care center. She was extremely nervous as we talked and again insisted that we sit on a park bench for privacy.

When I first started going to work after my training my parents had to go back to Ecuador to see about my father's land, and I didn't know what to do with my younger son. I didn't want to go back to work when my children were so young, but I had to. And since I didn't have anyone responsible to take care of my son, I had to get him into a day care center.

You know when I was being trained at Manpower I learned so much about so many things. When I went to Manpower for the training and I told the counselor what my husband's income was, they told me that he made too much and that I could not go into the program. He worked two jobs at that time. So the man that I was talking to, he must have dealt with these issues all the time, he told me that he was going to put down that my husband made only so much a week because otherwise I would not be qualified for the program. And I thought that was very nice of him to tell me that and to do that for me.

Then afterward when I got finished with the Manpower program I tried to get my children into a day care center so that I could go to work. My counselor at Manpower and I—we tried four or five day care centers but my income was too high. You know, it's terrible the way the society has things set up so that if you make a little money—my husband was making a hundred and twenty dollars a week in both jobs at that time and you know after taxes how much that is—you can't get into programs. You have to be on welfare or you have to be separated in order to get into a day care center, and my counselor, he told me that what I had to do was I had to say that I was separated. I had to put my husband out of my life and I had to tell them that he only gave me sixty dollars a week. He only gave me twenty or thirty dollars more than that a week, really.

So she called up the day care center for me and she told them that I was separated and what my husband gave me. I couldn't do it myself because I was shaking too much. *(She puts her hands out in front of her and starts shaking.)* And that is how I got my two older children into a day care center but I don't want anybody to know this. The day care center or anybody. I felt so badly that I had to do such a thing. I wish I didn't have to do anything like that but I had to go to work and it was the only way I could get them into a center. I wish that I would not have to lie and that I would not have to worry when we walk along the streets that maybe somebody would see us together. I wish I could have a life and live it freely.

You know, there should be free day care centers just as there are free schools for older children. If you go to high school nobody asks if you're married or single or how much you earn. It's free and it's for everybody. There should be day care from three or four years on for everybody even if you're not on welfare.

I think it's a terrible thing when people go on welfare. I never wanted to go on welfare even though they told me at the Center that I could. I feel and my husband feels that if you have your two good hands to work with that you should work.

Maybe it's that I have too much pride, but I see all around me these young people who are on welfare. They stay at home all day long. The city needs money so badly that they should put all those people on welfare to work. But, you know, they make people lie. A lot of people lie and say that they aren't married or that they are separated. What I would most prefer would be to stay at home and keep my children at home with me until they go to school and then to go out to work. And if my husband came home regular hours then I could work in the evening or take my courses in the evening. But actually I like working four hours a day. That's just right.

No, I don't pay anything at the Center for the day care. If I told them my real income I would have to pay fifty dollars a week per child and then I would be paying much more than I was making. It would be impossible. We need for my husband to work and for me to work in order to live a decent life.

You know, sometimes I think that when my children are out of the day care center I will go back and I will tell them the truth. I go back and forth in my own mind. I can't decide whether I should do that or whether I shouldn't do that. It might make it harder for other people. But, you know, I feel so guilty about lying to them. I feel so bad about it.

A few days later Maria told me how upset she had been when the director of the day care center asked her if she would talk with me.

When Mrs. Parker asked me if I would speak to you, I didn't know what to do. I could have told you the same story but somehow I chose not to—I chose to tell you the truth. But last night I didn't sleep all night worrying about what I told you. I was up at five o'clock in the morning ironing. But, you know, you have to tell somebody. I felt so badly about keeping my husband out of everything that I didn't want to do it anymore. If I was going to be in a book I didn't want to keep him out of it. I didn't want to pretend that I was doing it by myself. I did not want to look like a—how do you say it—a heroine or like a victim. I am neither a heroine nor a victim.

When my husband came here he had to struggle too. He was my high school teacher in Ecuador. He taught art. He's ten years older than I am. We went out for a year when I was still in Ecuador and we were in this country for about five years before we got married. When he came here he had to work as a bus boy—he didn't have any English—and then he worked as a porter in an apartment building. You know, it's especially hard because a teacher in Ecuador is very well respected and he used to be a very well dressed man. It was heartbreaking to see him at a job like that—being a porter. But then he decided that he needed to go into his own field even if he made less money. He went into commercial art but he had to begin at the bottom because he didn't know much about commercial art. So he was making about eighty dollars a week.

At that time he also took a second job so he would leave the house at seven o'clock in the morning and not come back until twelve or one in the morning. He never saw his children except on the weekends. And, you know, that isn't right, to see your children only two days a week. But then he got laid off of his second job because a computer replaced him, and it was at this time that he got many big debts. He found it very hard to get a second job that was only five or six hours, because to work another full eight-hour job was really too much. That is when I decided that I would have to go to work in order to pay off some of these debts because I was afraid that they would take the house from us.

And, you know, when I started to work it was very hard for me because my son was not being properly cared for by the person who was taking care of him. When I found out I was very upset and in tears all the time. Up till then I was working mornings, from nine to one. After that I requested that my hours be changed from twelve to four, and that solved part of the problem. Soon after, I asked the day care center if he could also attend. This was the only way I felt a little more relaxed going to work. I knew that my son was being properly cared for, both physically and emotionally.

I think that the role of a married woman is to care mainly for her home but once that is done, if she does not neglect her home and her children, I think that it is perfectly all right for her to go out and get a job and work and defend herself. Because what if something should happen to her husband? What if he should get sick or die or something should happen or they get separated? Sometimes women get grouchy or bored being home all the time and then they get cranky with their children. I know I can't sit around and do nothing. I get nervous. I think it's good for a woman to go out, but her primary responsibility should be in the home.

But my husband helps me. He helps me in the evenings when he comes home. Sometimes I'll ask him if he will read a book to the children, but usually he will say that he'll do something in the kitchen and he'll let me read the book to the children. He prefers that I do that sort of thing. And then I'll read to them. I like to read to them at night and then maybe lie down with each one of them for five or ten minutes and talk to them. Since I don't see them very much during the day I ask them what happened during the day and sometimes my daughter will start to cry and tell me about something that happened to her. And then by nine-thirty or ten we have everything done, the children are in bed, and then my husband will sit down and read or watch television and I will do my homework when I am in school.

No, I don't think that women's life is especially hard but I do think that there should be day care for everybody, especially for working women so that they don't have to worry about their children. One day I was at work and my children were sick and couldn't go to school. During the day I called them up and they answered the telephone and said they were alone. The radio was on full blast and they were screaming. Then I called the baby sitter and she didn't answer and then I called my house again and there was no answer there either. And I was so upset because I was at work. Then I called home again and let it ring and ring and ring, and I reached my brother who had not yet gone to work. I told my brother to bring the children to school anyway. I didn't care how sick they were I wanted them in school.

The only time that I feel comfortable and know they're safe is when they're in the Center. And in the Center the children aren't only being taken care of physically but they're being taken care of mentally. While they play they're learning and they're developing their motor coordination. I think it's very important for them to be with other people so that they don't become too dependent upon their mother. I think day care should be available to everybody, working women and women who do not work. Even if I did not work I would want my children to go to a center for a few hours a day.

Several months after our first interview, Maria Perez and I met again. She told me what had happened in the interim. Because she and her son's teacher at the day care center were concerned that he seemed shy and somewhat withdrawn, the family was referred to a child psychiatrist affiliated with the hospital where Maria works. In telling the psychiatrist her son's history (material which should, of course, remain confidential) she felt that she needed to describe the family structure accurately including the fact that her husband was living at home and that she had been deceiving the day care center. Maria felt the psychiatrist could not really understand the tensions and pressures the family was under without knowing this. She described how difficult it was to tell her (the psychiatrist) both what she had done and how upset she felt about having lied to Mrs. Parker, the head of the day care center with whom she had always had a warm relationship. The psychiatrist then told her that unless Mrs. Perez told Mrs. Parker of the deception that she, the psychiatrist, would tell her.

She decided that she had to go to the Center herself. While it was extremely difficult for her to tell Mrs. Parker that she had lied to her, she stressed that she had felt it was necessary and that she felt better now that the deception was over. Mrs. Parker, in her role as administrator, could not keep the Perez family in the Center without charge once she knew the facts, for if city agencies that subsidize day care costs for families who cannot pay were to learn that the Center was aware of the deception this could then jeopardize the entire Center. As Maria had been forced by the ultimatum of the psychiatrist into telling the Center, so the Center was forced to insist that the Perez family pay the correct amount immediately or take the children out of day care.

Maria could not afford to pay fifty dollars per week per child and so removed them from the Center at the end of the month. She did not have other adequate arrangements for the children and, of course, did not want to give up her job, which she needed, enjoyed, and had struggled so hard to get. After filling in with stopgap arrangements for a few weeks, Maria found another school that would take the children for less money.

The anguish she felt throughout this experience was acute. She felt humiliated that she should have been in such a position, embarrassed and guilty at having deceived someone who had shown her friendship, and angry that she, who has tried to work rather than accept welfare, should have such a difficult time.

CHAPTER 6

Frances Meyers

You have to go day by day. If you can get up in the morning and get dressed and go to work, that's all that counts.

Frances Meyers is a short, plump, blond, Jewish woman in her early fifties. Although she is outgoing, talks easily, and has a quick laugh, which is often at her own expense, her face is deeply lined and she looks older than her years.

Her husband died nearly two years ago. She and her nineteen-year-old son live in a spotlessly clean four-and-a-half-room apartment on the fifteenth floor of a building that is part of a large, five-year-old complex. Essentially a city-within-a-city, this development houses 15,000 families and includes shops, banks, restaurants, schools—from primary school through college—parks, churches, and synagogues. Frances spends much of her time in her bright, modern L-shaped kitchen and dinette. The living room with its plastic-covered couch and chairs appears to be used infrequently except for watching television.

Frances Meyers earns something over $5000 a year as an educational assistant in a primary school, and an additional $2000 by selling clothes out of her home. Her son also contributes to the household expenses. She is just managing financially and is concerned that she will be laid off because of New York City's precarious financial situation and because many of the children currently enrolled in her school need bilingual paraprofessional help. Frances clearly reflects the anxiety and hostility that have been aroused by a combination of population shifts and job insecurity.

I'm what they call an educational assistant. I work in a program called "Strengthening Early Childhood." We take children out of classrooms to help improve their reading. I used to live there right down the block from the school and walk to work. Now, I have to take three buses.

I work with the teacher. She gives the reading lesson and we start to teach the kids the consonants and the vowels. Even though they're in first or second grade, they still don't know their letters. I would say it's a lower income bracket and it's getting more Spanish. It was predominantly white at the inception of the school, but as the years progressed, it became black. Then the Spanish started to come in, and now it's like about sixty percent Spanish and forty percent black. The white children you can count on one hand. I've been working there for ten years so I've seen the entire change. And not only that—when the middle-class population moved out, those families had one or two children, whereas when the other children came in, there were four, five, six children to a family—and the school became overcrowded. When I came into the school it was under-utilized, and we used to bus children in; now we are busing children out.

In teaching the children reading, they get all sorts of games, books, newspapers, pictures, whatever turns them on. We teach them a story like Goldilocks or something like that and each one plays a part. We tape it, and then we play it back, so that they can hear it. Of course, this is what they enjoy. It's something different than the ordinary just taking out a book and sitting down and learning it. Last year we were on a one-to-one basis but this year the program is state-funded, I think. I just heard that we're going to have ninety children, one teacher, and three paraprofessionals. That's a lot.

We alternate the children, because you know sometimes there's favoritism with a child, sometimes there is a lack of understanding, and sometimes you just don't like a child. But I love working with the children; you get a certain personal relationship.

Originally I started as a paraprofessional. That was working in the classroom—like being a maid in a sense to the teacher. Whatever the teacher wanted you to do you would do. If she wanted you to mark a paper, if she wanted you to work with a certain child or a couple of children, that's what you would do. The teachers resented it at first; they really didn't want it. You know why? Because they weren't equipped to tell us what to do, really. Many of them still do resent us; they feel you're taking jobs away from teachers. But, on the other hand, a lot of the paraprofessionals have gone to school and have become teachers.

But there is a laxity among many of the paraprofessionals; there's a lot of goof-off time. They come in—they want to get paid, so naturally they come in—and they have work to do, but they don't report, and the teacher has to sit on them. I have yet to see somebody fired. Whether they work or don't work, we all get the same pay. I mean, look, if someone is working, they should put their time in to benefit the children as far as education is concerned.

In our school, oh, I'd say there are roughly about twenty-five paraprofessionals, and only three are white—myself and two of my friends. We have a large group of bilinguals because we have a bilingual program, and we have a few blacks. Everybody is very opinionated, especially we girls. I myself, because I've worked in the field so long, I feel that you know how to do certain things, and when someone tells you how to do it, you resent it. But actually that isn't right, because you can always learn something from somebody else even though they're not a professional.

My girlfriend and I are easygoing because we don't argue. We take it and just put it aside. But it bothers us and like sometimes we discuss it amongst ourselves saying that one of the girls is very pigheaded. She's very cynical. In fact, one black girl, one of her own kind, said that she can't make up her mind whether she's white or black because she has . . . she comes from a better . . . her husband has a good job, and her child goes to a private school. So, as her kind has said, she's neither here nor there. There are tensions, yes, but since we work together so long, we manage to cope with these things because we know how. They are mostly kept under tow.

Yes, I feel that the language does hinder us as far as not being able to communicate with the Spanish, but I resent a lot of things that they have gotten. I don't feel that they are qualified, in a sense, to gain certain things. Just now many of the teachers who had worked a certain number of years were laid off, but the bilinguals are just starting to work two and three years and none of them were laid off. I resent it. When I heard a young bilingual teacher in the auditorium say she'd like to know whether she's working for the new contract or the old contract, well, many teachers aren't working at all! I don't say she doesn't have to know her rights, but I feel resentful for the fact that they are not laid off at all. We're being pushed aside—the black and the white—in favor of the bilingual, right? My teacher, my principal has asked for bilingual "paras" now because our community needs more paras, and gradually the whites will be pushed out completely.

Of course, eventually, if I'm not able to speak the Spanish or get along with the children, this means my job. Before you might be able to get a transfer from one school to another, but I doubt it now, because the cutbacks are citywide—not just one school. You see, when we originally started to work in the school as parents, it was a white, middle-class school and we worked with our own as well as other children; now the blacks and the Spanish have their own children, but the whites rarely have children in school there now. In fact, many of the personnel here were laid off, so regardless of where you are working, if you have your job, you're very fortunate. That's the bad part of the job.

Every year when you come back to school, you never know if you have a job or if you don't have a job. There isn't anything secure about it. That goes for during the year; you could be laid off then as well. And now, if I get an increase in pay, I'll still be decreased because I've been cut in hours, and yet I still have expenses to pay such as higher carfare, higher food, and all the other things that are going up. And my income has to spread itself over the whole year. See, when professionals work, they get paid on a twelve-month basis. We work hours—we just work the time we put in and that's it. But a city job is good because you get two weeks vacation, you get your Christmas vacation, your Easter vacation—you're out at three o'clock.

I started to work when I was eighteen. I went into the world and saw how the boss would flirt with the girls in the factory, or, you know. I worked as a bookkeeper in a book bindery starting at ten dollars a week. After ten years the book binder went out of business and then I went to work in a printing firm—all this was before I was married. After I was married I worked there a few years until a month before my son was born. Then when he started school I volunteered in the school; then I started with two hours and gradually it worked into more. This was pin money, extra money, since my husband was alive at the time, and I felt the need for work, not only for the money, but for occupying your mind. I couldn't see sitting home and entertaining women with small children.

Ever since my son walked into first grade I started to work in the school he was going to so that he knew where I was. I would be home at three o'clock when he would be home. I always felt that my child should know where his mother is, and I didn't feel that I should go back to the business world because I felt that the hours would be too long. And then I transferred in order to get more hours; I've only worked in those two schools. When you work in one particular school, it's hard to pick up roots after many years and keep changing. Even though basically children are all the same, and parents are similar, but still, it's nice to have roots. You know the people, you know the area, you feel comfortable.

Oh, I enjoy my work, I enjoy it, but I truthfully enjoy selling clothes more. I started many years ago just selling sweaters because I had the advantage of meeting someone that worked for a knit place and that was also extra pin money. But then, in the past few years when I moved here, my husband became ill, and I needed the money, so I went in on a bigger and better basis. But only with the idea that I could buy on consignment so that I wouldn't have to lay out any money; I only pay for the clothes when I get paid.

And this connects me with my school; I'll tell you how. The teachers love to buy clothes, so I take my shopping bag and bring clothes to work and I have a lot of buyers. I sell a pantsuit for thirty-five dollars that would sell in a store for about forty-five dollars. I sell in the house, too, because, as I said, I have a lot of friends, so I give a friend a call and tell her I have a nice suit for her, and would she like to come up? I do enjoy it. I wish I could get more. I like fashions, I like colors, and I enjoy people coming up to the house; it's conversation and it's time-consuming, and I like hearing about the families and what they do and where the children are going and different stories about their jobs and things like that.

It gives me another reason for keeping my house nice. I always did like my house nice but this gives me more of a reason to do it. You see, before, my husband used to do a lot, and I was more a lady of out-going ways. He used to do the cleaning and the basics—the pots and the pans—and it was a big help. Many times I was embarrassed by saying that, because everybody felt—I thought that people would think that he was hen-pecked or something like that. But he enjoyed it; I never did. I always enjoyed business. I always enjoyed doing things and being with people. It always kept me on the go.

But as you get a little older, it's a little harder. I mean, now I would still like to get back into the business world but, the fears of going—I'm not afraid of the trains, but, I mean, going downtown every day is an extra hour traveling back and forth, as you get older you look to decrease your hours not to increase the hours as far as working. I enjoy school and I have to have a steady income so it's held me there for all these years. And I have accumulated a great deal of sick leave because I don't like to stay out unless I'm really sick. I can carry it on. I do carry it on, but we always have that fear of losing the job. And if I'm laid off, unless I go to another city job, the hours are just gone. Just lost. And I'm over fifty—I was fifty-three on my last birthday so of course I worry about getting another job.

I was born in the East Bronx near the Simpson Street Station. We only lived there a few years, and then when I was two-and-a-half we moved to a farm in Lakewood, New Jersey. My father worked, he was a hat maker, and at that time he made a lot of money. He thought that it would be good for my mother to be out of the city, so actually he worked in the city and made the money whereas my mother spent the money on the farm. He would come in only like once in two weeks, and he would send the money to my mother.

I didn't see him that much. My mother, my brother, my sister, and I lived on the farm. I'm the youngest. My brother was ten years older than I was, and my sister was five years older than I was. My brother has since passed away; my sister is still living. We only lived there a few years. My mother became very ill and she was in a hospital for a couple of years, and my father had to sell the farm.

Then we moved to the city, back to the same building where I was born. We stayed there a while and then we were split up. I lived with an aunt for a couple of years, my sister was at another place, and my brother was with some other relatives. It took a couple of years until we were able to get back together again. Then we moved to the West Side—at that time, we felt that it was an improvement—and my father bought a candy store. As my brother got older my father wanted a larger income, so we bought a larger candy store. In this interim my mother was home and then she was away. I didn't have my mother home very much. That was one of the things I felt lacking in raising a child, because I didn't really know very many things about rearing a child at this stage. My sister was like my mother; she took care of us. She cooked and tended to all the chores in the house in addition to working in the store.

My mother has been in and out of the hospital for many years. She's still alive, but she has been in the mental institution for thirty-three years. It's like a living hell; a person's really better off dead. The last time she went into the hospital was thirty-three years ago.

You see, when she originally went into an institution, they experimented as far as mental illness. They would take out your teeth; they would give a woman a hysterectomy. All these were things that were experiments in a sense to see if the person would come back to their normal self—and maybe you did, maybe that helped—I really don't know for sure if that was the reason that she was able to get home. But the last time she became very ill, it was from a sunburn out in Rockaway. She had a very bad sunburn and became mentally deranged—you know, where she would carry on screaming and become very depressed and want to kill herself and things like that. And for many years I used to visit quite frequently—at least once a week. It's very hard. It's your own parents, but you just cannot face—only a person who goes through this can realize that after a while—I won't say you're numb—but the visits became very decreased. Especially in the last few years after I had been married and all that.

I don't remember seeing my mother when I was small and going to visit her. I imagine my father did. I can honestly say I remember my mother home very little. Very little. I remember one scene when an ambulance came to take her away because she was ready to commit suicide. She wanted to jump out of a top floor window. My son doesn't know anything about this. He knows his grandmother is ill, and we had taken him there in the car, you know, as a ride. And once when he'd gotten into his teens, we took him inside a little bit. But, I'd say, for the past three years I haven't taken him. I don't think it's fair to subject him to seeing his grandmother. Literally, she's a basket case. She had a stroke and she isn't able to walk. She has to be put and tied into a wheelchair when she sits up, and the sights around her are not too much better.

Not too long ago, after the cuts in the budget, I received a letter from the hospital saying that I would have to take her home. I, you know, I didn't know what to do. So I called up and they said, "Well, under the circumstances it isn't advisable for her to go." They recommended that she stay there.

I certainly couldn't manage to maintain her. I can hardly maintain myself. She doesn't know my father passed away—she knows and speaks very little. She still asks, though, why she can't go home. Not that she knows where home is. She doesn't know that I only have one child; she doesn't know that my brother has passed away, and that his wife has passed away. She doesn't know that she has four beautiful grandchildren. I feel the only thing that keeps her alive is that she doesn't have the economic problems that all of us living outside do. She doesn't know what money means or about the need for money. Her heart must be strong in order for her to put up with all this for so many years. And to be in surroundings where there are so many people of various and different mental conditions. I truthfully haven't gone for over a year right now, because I had so many problems with my husband.

I went through a similar situation with my husband. Unbeknownst to me, all of a sudden he would have a breakdown where he wasn't able to go to work. Physically he looked like a big strapping man; mentally he could not get himself out of bed to go to work. He was depressed, and I would take him to the psychiatrist. I don't—I really don't know how—well, I—I went to my medical doctor first, and he would try to help me by giving me some sort of drugs for my husband but after the drugs did not work, he suggested that I take him to a psychiatrist. I was always supposed to be the strong one, and I took him.

The first time I took him to the psychiatrist, I took him through a clinic. Anyone who has been to a clinic and has seen, not seen, but heard the shock treatment would think that they were in a snake pit, literally. He would become okay after a few treatments. He was able to regain everything he had lost as far as being able to go to work, and it was, like, forgotten. But after the first time he became ill, I would always—every morning I would have the fear of his not being able to get up to go to work. It seemed to subside after a couple of years and then there would be a recurrence. Out of twenty-two years of marriage, he had five breakdowns like that.

After the first time at the clinic, I decided if I had to get money somehow or other, I would take him privately, and it was coincidental that I took him to the same psychiatrist privately, the same one who had worked in the clinic two days a week. It was only the fifth time that I went to him that I finally said to him, "Well, what brings this on? There must be something that makes a person—what sort of mental sickness is this? I mean, there must be some name for it?" And he said it was "self-inertia." In other words, brought about by his self, worrying about how he's going to pay his bills due to economic conditions.

He was a taxi driver. He enjoyed his work because he met many people, and a stranger would think that he was a comedian. He was very happy-go-lucky, and he would make everybody laugh. He was a Jekyll and Hyde. Only I knew what the other self was. He was a very good man as far as being a good husband and a good father, but he was mentally weak. His first episode was when my son was born. My son was only an infant—I think he was about a little over a year—and my husband became ill and I had to take him—I tried everything...I...I...He didn't want to go to doctors—he didn't believe in spending a lot of money on doctors and he felt that he would go to the V.A.* He was there for a while, and he walked out. He felt that he was in a snake pit and that he could help himself. It just was a matter of time and my patience in order for him to come to himself. And this did happen. After he got out of the V.A., it was just a question of how long I could take these periods, five, six weeks, two months, when he would just sit around.

He was always a big eater. When he stopped eating, I knew he didn't feel well. He tried to occupy himself with doing things in the house, because he did not like to face anybody in the street. That was his only symptom, his not wanting to go out in the street. It was a fear of them asking him questions about why he wasn't working or why he was home. He would say to me he doesn't feel well, that he can't explain the feeling, but he just begged me to take my time and have patience with him and understand that he's not acting, that it's just something that comes over him, and that he's not able to go to work.

I suppose I didn't understand a lot of these things, but now when I think back, I suppose I was pretty patient, too. And being able to tolerate all this, I felt, well, all this is part of marriage. And, you know, if I was to become ill, hopefully he would've done the same thing. It was very hard. Especially with the kid. It was like (crying) a double, double dose, so to speak. When my son was small (hesitantly, crying), I guess I didn't speak very much to my son. My kid is a quiet kid. That's why I say, in rearing him, only because of working in schools and being close with the children that I realized—excuse me, I'm sorry—the love that the mother has for her child.

I really wasn't a demanding person. I would always insist my husband have a vacation every year and go to some immedi-

---

* Veterans Administration hospital.

ate vicinity—Atlantic City or Washington—something for both of us to enjoy, to see, and divert ourselves from the home grounds, 'cause I always felt that would give everybody a pick-up. In fact, today I still feel that the only thing for me to look forward to is a vacation. Otherwise you become sort of in a rut.

In addition to being mentally ill, he had two heart attacks so it was a constant. The first time he had a heart attack was eight years ago, before we moved here, and he was only out of work for a short period of time. Little did I realize that the doctor had said to him to stay out as long as possible to gain his strength back. Even though he was a cab driver, it still requires a certain amount of strength and tension, and emotion is drained.

Since I had gotten married at a late date, we both had a few thousand dollars, and it was only because of the savings that we were able to go over these hurdles. I wasn't working until my son was in the first grade, and my husband's income wasn't that great where I could save money. That's why I always had a fear of spending money because I always felt that if he became ill, I would have to have at least five hundred to a thousand dollars to tide me over for the doctors. Well, once I started to work I was lucky I worked for the city. The coverage was there. It didn't pay all the doctors' and hospital bills, but it did cover a great deal.

The feeling of being left without money is just—is just—to this day when I don't have any money in my wallet I'm very insecure. Of course, due to him leaving a small insurance policy, that helps a little bit to relax my mind. Still, how long does a small insurance policy last? But, I, I don't have the fear of such an exorbitant doctor bill. I mean, I have hospitalization coverage. Now my worry is for my son to have coverage where he's working; he doesn't have this insurance yet at work so I have to pay for these on the outside.

We had lived here approximately a year when he had his second heart attack, and he was taken to a hospital where, I must say, he had the most wonderful care, intensive care. He came home and he was home like say about eight or nine months when he had another attack and he was taken to another hospital. There the doctor wanted to send him right home, but through my insistence he went to the convalescent part of the hospital. He needed care and I felt the longer I prolonged his convalescence, the better it was for him as well as for myself. I had to work, and when he came home, to have my piece of mind, I hired a woman sitter to prepare certain meals for him. I knew he was very ill, and yet I, I guess I didn't want to realize it that much either. And he only had her for a short time, because he insisted he could manage for himself.

Now he was told that he shouldn't smoke, but I knew he would take a cigarette here and there. And then he was taken to the hospital again, and I had him at the cardiologist and then he was fine when all of a sudden he didn't feel well. The cardiologist couldn't get to the house and they said to take him to the hospital, and I called the emergency service. Anyway, later my husband was in bed and he said that he had to go to the bathroom, and he said, "You know, there's something funny—my mother always said when your ears are not red that you are not well." And he said he loved me very much for my patience and understanding, and he said he had to go to the bathroom (*struggling not to cry*).

I took him to the bathroom and when he went back to bed, he laid down on the bed, and he just closed his eyes. I was alone. I knew in a sense he wasn't here. I wouldn't believe it and I called—there is a detective on the floor and I knew if he could get any help quickly, he would do it. He came in and I guess he knew it, too, but he tried to pacify me and he said he'd call the police emergency, which he did, and they came with the oxygen and all that, and he was D.O.A. Because he passed away in the house, I had to have him in the house practically all the day because we had to get the death certificate. When I called the cardiologist to get the death certificate, he asked—he asked me what happened. I said, "I really couldn't tell you as all I know is my husband isn't here."

I guess I was in shock for quite a few months, but I kept going, or making the motions anyway. I don't know what it is, but that drive to just keep going is, thank God, it's there. And I think—why, why sit back? I—I'm not old enough to retire or sit back, so what is there to sit back for? There is so much to see, there is so much to know, so many things to learn, so we keep going.

I kept myself busy after my husband passed away. He died December 15 two years ago. That was a big stepping stone, to be head of the household all of a sudden, 'cause I always felt that I had someone even though he wasn't extremely strong, but it was very important to have someone else with you. I enjoy people; it's nice to know how other people are doing, and it's nice to have friends, to have the phone ring. Occasionally they invite you to go out and have dinner. Sometimes the boob tube gets a little boring.

How did I meet my husband? That's an interesting question. I was introduced to my husband. My sister's father-in-law lived in his building, and her step-mother-in-law was a type of person that always introduced people, and she had wanted to introduce my husband to me about six or seven years previously but he didn't want to meet me because he said he didn't want to go with a short girl. Well, that was seven years previously. But after seven years he decided he might try a date.

We met in January and that August we were married. It was fast. Well, we both weren't youngsters. My husband was twenty-nine, I think; I was twenty-eight. I was a little hesitant at first. He had some money so I felt that he wasn't—I don't know how to explain that—a fly-by-night, but he really wasn't set with a career of any kind. My husband was in the fruit line and he worked for people and I didn't realize that he didn't like to take orders, didn't like to listen to anybody. I really didn't see his entire true nature. I knew he had a very bad temper, but only when somebody would step on him. Otherwise, he was always like a kitten. He was very easygoing and all, but if somebody did something to hurt him, he would want to do anything to get back at them regardless of the length of time it took.

But he had an ideal—he had a dream, an ideology. He felt Russia was Shangri-la; he felt it was heaven. They didn't have to worry about ten or fifteen dollars for a pair of shoes—it wasn't competitive, and everybody worked. He believed in their medical services and in their educational system. I felt that socialism was my belief. I could sooner see socialism than communism, but he felt that communism was the ideal way of living. I thought he was, like, dreaming, and I didn't want him to wake up because I felt this would destroy him completely.

Many times we went to people's homes and this was a topic of conversation. There are a few people that might agree with him, but I didn't want it to get to a point where every time we went any place that this was the main discussion. So to avoid this, he would always tell stories. Since he was a cab driver there were many incidents with actors and actresses and the different jokes about them. At times I felt that people were using him as an actor to be on the stage and get the conversation off themselves in a sense. At times I resented it. Just a few intimate friends actually knew him from the other side.

I don't know too much about his background. I knew he was a good son, but I didn't realize how much out of eight children his mother hovered over him. In fact, his sisters resented him in some ways because of the partiality his mother had for him. I'd say he lived in a good home, he always did everything for his mother or his father, and he always worked, so this was one of the reasons why I felt he probably would be reliable as a husband and as a father. But it was only after I was married that I realized his emotional instability.

I think—sometimes I wonder at my stability. I wouldn't say stability, but I mean—in fact, I find myself the past two weeks getting slightly depressed—not depressed, I wouldn't put it that way, but low (crying).

My girlfriend's husband came up. He always likes to converse with me. He mentioned the fact that I had been engrossed in my husband's life all these years, protecting him and shielding him from many problems. That was one of the reasons I didn't want to take a job as a bookkeeper again because I felt that if I made more money than he did it would degrade him. And in doing this, I really submerged myself. As I kept talking to him, I think I felt myself sinking into this low feeling. But it's not a continuous thing. It's partly a lack of social life. I love the idea of seeing my friends, I love the idea of going different places, but I'm low in the sense of having a companion.

My son is a doll, but he's extremely opposite to my husband in some ways. First of all, he's a young boy; he's only nine-teen, and his trade—he's a mechanic at a gas station. In fact, I tried to get him to go to school for mechanics, 'cause I always felt that white piece of paper meant the difference between a couple of zeros or not, but I just couldn't get him to the idea of staying in school. He's been working for two years and he en-joys it. He makes a nice living and he contributes a great deal of money towards the house, but I'm not used to dirt. My husband was meticulous. It's a constant cleaning, picking up, and things like that *(crying)*. I'm sorry, I don't mean to. Every once in a while it just goes against me. Even his laundry, you know, the handkerchiefs with the grease and the oil. But it's his choice and he's happy; he likes what he's doing; he makes money. And then I find him going into the same pattern as my husband—when he works late he gets tired, comes home, he eats, and then just watches television.

But what keeps me going is that I'm really not as bad off at all as other people, but between the rent strike at the place you live and the possibility of being laid off at the job, it is depress-ing. Yes, there's a rent strike. We won't pay the rent increase; it was at least a twenty-five to thirty percent increase. We're pay-ing our old rent. There are fifteen thousand families in the de-velopment and over twelve thousand are with the strikers be-cause when we moved here the original plan was twenty-seven dollars a room, and now it's going up to fifty and sixty dollars a room. There are many instances where husbands and wives are working, but one third of the people are senior citizens and live on fixed incomes. The strike has been going on since June and this is October, and it doesn't look like it'll finish.

I'm now paying two hundred and twenty-two dollars for four-and-a-half rooms and garage space. It's a reasonable amount of money, and the reason I say that is because it includes gas and electric, and in the summer there's central air conditioning and that's included, too. Now, salaries have gone up and with the increase the rent would have gone up to two hundred and seventy-five dollars which would have been bearable; however, we've been getting an increase every year. It will be five years since we moved in. The original contract was for one hundred and thirty-five dollars, but before we moved in, we got an increase and paid one hundred and fifty-seven dollars and then within five years it'll be almost double. And my income has decreased quite a bit.

I enjoy living here. There are many clubs, there are many facilities, and there are many people. I have a friend in every other building. When you are a widow you find that many people don't ask you to go to different places. I know when my husband was alive, I had a friend downstairs that was a widow, and if ever we would go to the beach or some sort of a place like that we always took her along. I'm fortunate in the sense that I have a friend downstairs who's like that. It's not that I always go, but it's nice to be asked. I have another couple in another building that constantly asks me to go out to dinner with them on Sunday to the Chinese restaurant or something like that, and to me it's important.

But like I said, there are times when there is a blank, when it's raining on a Sunday or something like that, and my son is sleeping. I do my laundry Sunday morning, but that only takes an hour, an hour-and-a-half, and then I hate hanging around waiting for him to get up to give him breakfast. I try to get something to do. I absorb myself with the paper for an hour or two in the morning to keep myself up to date. But sometimes you feel that you just want to change completely, and I found hopefully the only best change for anyone is getting a vacation. So I'm going to a hotel in the mountains with a girlfriend for a weekend the end of October.

Women's lib? I believe in women's lib to a point. I feel where a job is concerned that a woman should certainly get the same salary, and if a girl feels that she wants to be a truck driver that's her prerogative. And why couldn't a woman be a coal miner if she so wishes? There shouldn't be any restrictions if the party feels she is willing to do these types of jobs. I can see that a man can concentrate in the subject he takes up or on his work, whereas a woman whether she works or doesn't work has responsibilities at both ends. I feel that a man should cooperate in half of the amount of work that's in the home, but not everybody is cut out that way. It really is up to the two individuals.

I've seen some liberal women who affect me as being a little disappointed with certain things, whether it's a man or whether it's with their occupation, some sort of disappointment in a sense, and feel that it's like a vengeance—that they want to become so recognized, and this is why they speak out.

But I don't think women are as oppressed as they were years ago. I think there's a larger field, but I still feel that there could be more fields open to them. And I don't feel that a woman is only to bear children; I don't think that's her principal role. I feel that if a woman wants to be a doctor, a lawyer, or an Indian chief, this is her prerogative, and I don't think she should be held back.

I don't see how any woman with any ounce of brains could stay in the house continuously unless she does something to occupy her time. Any woman who just stays in, cooks and cleans and does the necessities of a home, it's not—oh, I don't know, it becomes very dull. There's nothing to learn, nothing to see, no one to speak to and compare different topics.

I went to work just for the time my child was in school and it was just to occupy myself for a short time. If I had been able to pay someone to take care of him part-time, I would have done it. But I couldn't afford it financially, so I had to compromise. And the reason that I wanted to stay home with my son when he was young was because I didn't have my mother home. I don't say that I recommend it for other women, but I felt this was my way of looking at things. Had I had a different childhood, I might not think the same. Especially, being of the Jewish faith, it was the mother that was in the home.

But, you know, you never can tell what will happen. The other day my son saw me looking at the paper about this rent strike situation and he said, "Gee, Mom, you think we'll have to move?" And I said, "Well, so long as both of us work, we'll see that we hold on, together. But, as you get older, and you decide to move out, and you meet a girl—I'll worry about it then." I just can't think that much ahead. You have to go day by day. If you can get up in the morning and get dressed and go to work, that's all that counts.

Since the time of these interviews, Frances has left her job in the school system and has gone to work for a Jewish social-service agency as a clerical worker. When I last saw her, the union she belonged to had been on strike for several weeks and she was extremely upset about losing so much pay in exchange for what she though would, in all likelihood, be insubstantial gains.

During this time her son had become engaged and subsequently was married, so Frances has moved to a one-bedroom apartment in the same complex. She was very anxious about his upcoming marriage for, while she felt she should be happy for her son and his fiancée, she dreaded being alone and feared the depression that she had anticipated and was now feeling. In spite of her many friends and the number of activities available in her immediate environment, she, who has described herself as a "lady of outgoing ways," said that now she felt isolated and alone.

CHAPTER 7

Rose O'Rourke

I moved in here in 1943 right after we were married. My son wants me to move to the suburbs near them in the worst way. He's after me every day, but I feel that I'll have no friends if I move out there . . . Here I have some neighbors . . . I have relatives . . .

Rose O'Rourke is a sixty-eight-year-old widow who emigrated from Ireland to this country at the age of nineteen. She works part-time as a waitress in an executive dining room on Wall Street. On the day I first met her, Rose greeted me warmly in the hallway at the top of the stairs leading to her fourth-floor apartment. She wore a purple wool dress with an apron tied around her waist, her gray hair was softly waved, and she wore tortoise-shell glasses with a few sparkles along the upper rim.

Rose lives alone in a five-story walk-up across the street from an auto repair shop in a neighborhood with other older buildings, newer two-family, brick, semi-attached houses, and a few shabby shops. Her fifty-year-old apartment building has distinctly seen better days; its large entrance hall has tile floors and a high ceiling with the remnants of what must have been a massive and elaborate light fixture.

She pays $142.00 per month for her spacious four-room apartment. The walls of the long, narrow kitchen are painted gray, the floor is gray, and the white appliances are functional though not modern. Both her bedroom and living room are furnished with heavy, somewhat worn, traditional mahogany furniture. A black cat sleeps on the couch. Hanging on the wall by her front door is a framed certificate honoring her husband for his "devoted service" during the Second World War; it is signed by Richard Nixon, and Rose says it simply came in the mail one day after her husband died four years ago.

The O'Rourkes had one child, a son, who lived at home until he married a year ago. He and his wife now live in the suburbs, and Rose is yet another elderly parent remaining in the city while her children move out in search of safety and schools. Her son has been trying to persuade her to move out of the city nearer to them, but she prefers to stay near her friends.

Rose O'Rourke is a warm, friendly woman who talks easily but sparingly with a light Irish brogue.

I grew up in Ireland, in the West of Ireland. I was the oldest of seven children and I came here in 1928 when I was nineteen. I had a couple of uncles here, and my aunt came back to visit with the children when I was about seventeen and she brought me out two years later. Then my sister came about a year afterwards. And we have had it pretty nice, you know.

There was a lot of trouble in Ireland back in that time with the Republican Army and the Free State Army. A lot of trouble, but I didn't know very much about it. We came because we were poor. I mean we didn't have a lot of money and we were seven children.

My father was a farmer. We had quite a big farm, a family farm. We grew all kinds of vegetables: potatoes, corn, wheat, and all that. My father went to work in England and Scotland a lot because there weren't many jobs in Ireland. Sometimes he'd be gone for nine or ten years. And my mother was home with us children. There were fourteen years between the oldest and the youngest so my mother had a baby every two years. She didn't have it easy. She used to work the farm herself; she would hire somebody to do a lot of the work for her, and we used to help her, too. We were four boys and four girls, and there was one child older than me that died. It was very hard; we couldn't grow enough food to sell and whatever money we had came from my father. Everything that had to be done on the farm I did; that's why I never liked the country.

I went to the sixth grade in school. Some of them went further; one of my brothers went to the eighth grade. They wanted him to go on for higher education, but I don't know if he did.

So the two of us came here, but you know what happened then? They stopped the immigration coming here during the Depression years so some of my family went over to England. I have two brothers and two sisters in England. I saw them four years ago when I went there for my mother's funeral. My mother had been living in England, too. I had been there about four years before that and that was the first time I had seen my mother in forty years. I found a big change. You know, I thought I should see my mother like I saw her when I left home; she was a young woman then. And now she was about eighty-two and had gotten heavy and all that. No, no, I never had any regrets about coming here.

Oh, when I was planning to come to New York I thought it was going to be beautiful, and it was. The city was beautiful then. Today it's a slum. Then the streets were clean; the subways were clean; everything was clean. You wouldn't see dust anywhere. No broken down buildings—nothing like that. It was lovely. And I had a wonderful aunt and uncle. They were very good to me.

When I first came here I lived out for a while, took care of children. I always had a job. I didn't make big money, but I worked during the whole Depression. I worked for different families. I worked for one family down on 72nd Street for about seven years and I still keep in contact with them. They live in a lovely big apartment. I go down there to see them—the mother and the daughter. The husband is dead. Oh, the mother's about seventy-five, and she's a lovely person. She originally comes from Boston. In fact for the holidays now I must make an Irish soda bread and bring it down to her. She loves that.

Then in 1939 I went to work in Schrafft's. It was hard work, but I was young and I enjoyed it. You know when you're young you can do anything. I used to work from eleven in the morning to eight at night and some days from twelve to nine. Those days we used to make about ninety dollars a week and most of it was tips. Those days that was very good money.

Then I got married in 1942; my husband was in the service. He was from Ireland, too, and I met him at a party one night. His whole family was here. They were rather comfortable on the other side, and then the father died and they lost everything, so they all came out here in 1926. He was a very, very fine man, my husband. Tall and heavy set, nice looking, very nice looking. I miss him an awful lot.

I worked at Schrafft's for eight years, and when I got pregnant with my son I quit and I lost my seniority, so when I went back to work I had to start new again. You know, there was no union, not in those days. I stayed home for six years. And during that time I lost another one or two children, and I wasn't so young anymore and I took a very bad hemorrhage and they had to operate on me. Then two years after I had the operation I went back to work. The doctor told me that it was good for me to get out of the house and go back to work. I would be much better off, he said. So I went back to work and I'm still working. Bill was in second grade and I used to send him to summer day camp; he used to come home so tired that it made me feel bad about going back to work. My husband used to say, "Oh stay home, Rose." But it was good working—you get in with a different crowd of girls and there was always somebody with a good joke. When I was home I missed all the girls, all the fun we'd have, and I was tied down with a child which made it very hard.

I stayed there for two years, and then they were opening those executive dining rooms all over and they were asking the girls who would like to go to work down there, so I said I'd go. It was much easier work and I figured, well, I only wanted to make pin money for myself, you know; I didn't expect to have to work all those years. I said, "I'll have money for spending, for clothes and shoes, and whatever I wanted to do." It was a very good move then. And I loved it. I loved it. I love to get out.

I still work in an executive dining room, in a bank down on Wall Street with four girls, and we're kept busy. They have a cafeteria and they have a dining room. We serve lunch in the dining room every day for the executives. We work from twelve o'clock to two—two hours. Then we clean up and we come home. I get home around four o'clock in the afternoon. Twenty hours a week. Twenty-two years I've been working twenty hours. That was enough for me when my husband was living, but now I'm on Social Security. I took Social Security when I was sixty-two and I get along on Social Security and what I make. When I retire—I plan to retire in the spring—I'll get a pension of some kind; it might be a small pension, but I'll get something from the union.

I feel I have worked long enough; I'd like to get out now. Sometimes I get tired—not at work, in the morning. I find it hard to get up. Yesterday morning I got up very early—I got up at a quarter after five. I was working a full day. I had to work breakfast and I worked a full day. But last night I wasn't tired; I went to visit a friend of mine who just came out of the hospital and I got home here about half past ten.

When I retire I'll be tight with money; I know that. I get my husband's Social Security which is three hundred and nine dollars and then I make about two hundred dollars a month myself. That's what I get tax free, so it isn't too bad. We pay eight dollars and fifty cents a month union dues. I guess maybe at the end, when I'll be getting a little pension, it will be worth it to me. But the younger generation that's starting out, I don't think they should stay in this kind of work. They should go in for more money, get different jobs. I know if I was young again, I wouldn't stay in this field. My sister was a widow when she was twenty-eight, she had two children, and she was a telephone operator. When she retired at sixty-five, she got a lovely pension, she gets free telephone, she gets a very good Social Security, so she's fine.

I enjoy the job because it gets me out of the house a couple of hours a day. Because it can be very lonesome in the house. I usually try to get out a lot. The holidays are very bad—Thanksgiving, Christmas, Easter, and the New Year—'cause I always used to have a lot of company around the holidays and now so many of them are dead. My sister-in-law is dead, my brother-in-law is dead, the family is all scattered. And some of them have moved away to Jersey. So . . . My sister-in-law lives over on the West Side—I keep in touch with her. And my son comes in. He comes in.

My husband died four years ago. He was a bus driver at one time and then he was working up at the church, and one Sunday morning he went out to work and he died on the job. And the police came down here and told me; my son was gone to the beach. It was June 10—that was it. He was sixty-four years old. Wonderful man. We would have been married thirty-two years that July. Yes, yes, it's very hard. If he had been ill for a while or something like that, if I knew there was no cure for him—but one, two, three, he was gone. The heart. Although he had a perfect heart. It was a blood clot. No warning at all. No warning.

It was on a Sunday and I had just come back from church

and the bell rang downstairs. I answered down and I saw the priest coming and I thought it was my nephew 'cause I have a nephew a priest. I said, "Oh, here comes Father Jimmy, he's going to bring me some company and I'm not prepared." But he said, "I'm from St. Cecilia's." And I knew right away; I knew right away something had happened. I saw the policeman walking in back of him. And he was going to retire the following October.

I asked Rose why her husband had left his job as a bus driver to work at the church. She told me that he was turned in for an alleged theft of money.

Well, he was a very good man, and they used to have him check in the people at the back of the bus. I don't think they do it anymore. They gave him this clipper to clip the money in, and for him to get the people on the bus fast he used to slip the money in his bag and then check it all later on. And somebody turned him in and he lost the job. And he never took it. He checked it in with the machine later on when the rush was over. But they didn't give him a chance for nothing—nothing. And he worked for the bus company for forty years. I think if he had gotten a good lawyer, he would have been able to fight it but he never got a lawyer. He thought the union would help him but the union didn't help. When he was dead, I was talking to one of the men that worked with him and he said, "I worked with Mike a long time—and I know he checked every penny of that money. He checked the whole thing."

I told him he should get a lawyer, and he didn't do anything about it. I guess he figured he didn't want to spend the money and he wouldn't win anyhow. But I think if he had gotten Paul O'Dwyer,* he would have done something for him. He lost his pension; he lost everything, and I get nothing from the bus company. Nothing. He was terribly upset about it. He was never the same after it happened. He brooded over it. He got a slight stroke at one time. Forty years of working and nothing in back of it. He blamed the bus driver; this bus driver didn't like

---

* A popular, highly visible, Irish-American, New York City political figure often involved in liberal causes.

him because he packed the bus too heavy, but I don't know. Nobody knows. It could be a spy, too. Someone from the bus company. He was terribly depressed. He never got over it— never, never got over it. Although he loved working up in St. Cecilia's, and the priests were very fond of him and all the people there loved him. He was a very lovable man. Too good, you know—very good-natured. That's why I feel so bad. If he had lived a little longer and had a little time to relax and retire, but he didn't. What are you going to do? You have to live and forget about it. It's the only thing I try to do. Forget about the whole thing. I manage.

I miss Bill though, an awful lot, now that he's out of the house. He's a wonderful boy. He lived here till he got married. He was a good home boy. He went to parochial school and from that he went to CCNY * and then he got his master's from CCNY in engineering. Last November he got married; he married a lovely girl and they're very happy.

When Billy was born, Mike and I set up a trust fund for him, and Mike said, "Put it in your name, I won't bother putting it in my name." So I put it in my name and Bill's. And all the money he used to get for birthday parties and Christmas and everything like that, we put in there. Every once in a while if Mike had given me too much money, I'd throw that in, too. When Bill graduated from high school he wanted a car. Mike said to me, "Give him the money, Rose." So, I said, "No. If he wants the car, let him go out and work for it." So when he was getting married, I told him and Sue that I wanted to see them some night. So they both came in; they didn't know what I wanted. I gave them the bankbook. I said, "This is money I saved for your college education. You went to CCNY so here's the money Daddy and I had saved for you." There was fifty-six hundred dollars. It was terrific. They were so happy. He never knew I had a penny saved for him, never knew. I handed the bankbook over to him. I said, "Daddy would want me to give it to you." They were shocked.

---

* City College of New York.

They're expecting a baby any day. I wish it were here now. His wife is a teacher, a very smart girl. She makes a very good salary, twenty-three thousand dollars a year. She's a special teacher for children that have problems. She wants to go back again to work after she has the baby, but I think, let me see, how would I put it now? I think she should stay home with her own baby for at least a year or two, to see it grow up a little. I think nobody can take the place of a mother with a child. What do you think?

Women's liberation? I don't know much about that stuff. I think they've done a good job. I think there are a lot of women already out working and they're doing a good job, but when their children are very young I think they should stay home with them. I really think they should. But, in general, I think it's good for them to get out and work. Very good. And it would be nice if they could afford to have somebody do the work for them. If the husband and wife were working and somebody could come in and clean the house and the mother do the cooking, I think that would be terrific. What about husbands helping? I don't know *(laughs)*. Some of them help and some of them don't. Some of them are not much good in the kitchen and around the house. My husband was terrific. Oh, he was terrific. He cleaned the house on his day off; he vacuumed; he'd do everything. But he couldn't cook and he couldn't shop. But give him a job cleaning the house—as a matter of fact I used to say sometimes that I wish he didn't work so hard, that he should sit down and rest, but whatever day he'd be off he'd say, "You don't have to worry about cleaning tomorrow, I cleaned the house today." Polish furniture. Do anything.

He used to meet me coming home from work. He'd come home around four o'clock and he'd meet me by the A & P and we'd do the shopping together. I'd do the shopping and he'd help me bring it in. Yes, we did divide the housework, and I think men should pitch in and help. Some of them won't do it though. Mike used to often say to me, "Why don't you stay home, Rose?" He said, "You don't have to work." I used to say to him, "I enjoy it, Mike." The couple of hours mean so much to me and the extra money was nice too.

I think it's good for women to work, I think it's wonderful. But I see all the Puerto Ricans around here going out to work every morning with their babies, taking them to baby sitters. Even the young girls with little babies in the cold weather. Well, I know I wouldn't do it unless I had to. Maybe they have to, you never know. Some of them don't make big salaries and everything is so expensive today; it's terrible.

This neighborhood used to be Jewish and German and Italian and Irish. The man that owned this house when I moved in here was German. Real German from the other side. Oh, it was a beautiful house. There was a big light with crystal coming down from the ceiling in the entrance hall. He brought it back from Germany with him. Oh, it was a beautiful building. Very strict. You couldn't stand outside the door to talk to anybody. You daren't stand in front of the door. They didn't allow it. Now it's going down. The halls are not kept as clean as they used to be. The supers we had here just moved and we got some Puerto Ricans and they don't keep the place as nice. Was there a lock on the door when you came in? There was? They're pretty good like that.

Oh yes, it's pretty safe. I don't worry. Although I was mugged down there in the hall one morning about four years ago. I know Mike was dead at the time. I was coming in from the store at twelve o'clock noon and this colored fellow came in back of me and put a knife in my back. Took all my money, took about a hundred dollars I had in my bag. I was scared for the time, but I got over it. I told him to take my bag. He said, "I don't want your bag, I only want your money." He made me turn my bag upside-down on the stairs. He was a young kid.

Well, what can I say? I watch myself when I'm coming in now. I look before I come in; I look around to be sure there's nobody following me. I look before I go upstairs and I have my key in my hand all the time. That day I was looking for the key in my bag and the package was in my arm. I'm careful now. Last night, for example, I went to seven-thirty mass not too far from here, a ten-minute walk. I left my pocketbook home. I just took my key and my rosary beads, that's all. Sometimes I walk up to see some friends of mine near here and I take the bus back, so I take my pocketbook with me. The bus lets me off down the block here.

There is a large development near here which is pretty well shot. They're mugging them left and right there. But there's an awful lot of people moving out—all the young people that have children. Anyone at all that can afford it, they're all buying houses. Young white people. Puerto Ricans and blacks are moving in. Mostly black. Now the nurse across the hallway from me—she's black—and I couldn't ask for a nicer person. Of course, she's from a very good culture. She has two brothers, both doctors, and a brother an engineer and her sister is the principal of a high school, so she has a very good background. If you get the good class of colored people, they're very good.

The Puerto Ricans—they don't pay their rent. There was a Puerto Rican family next door to me here—they just moved, and they were lovely. But they were working people, they were hard working people. Then we had a Puerto Rican family down on the ground floor. He was Puerto Rican, the girl was Jewish, and they were living together. They owed the landlord eight hundred dollars and he had to put them out. And she was a lovely looking girl. I don't know what she ever saw in him. If she wanted to go and live with a man I would go and live with a man who would support me and give me what I wanted and everything I needed. But she had nothing.

This is my first apartment. I had three rooms across the hall, and when Bill was getting bigger I got four rooms over here. I moved in here in 1943 right after we were married. Bill wants me to move to the suburbs near them in the worst way. He's after me every day, but I feel that I'll have no friends if I move out there. I'm going to miss all my friends because I don't drive, and it's very hard to get from there into the city. I'd be lost out there. Unless he gets a two-family house and he'd rent me one of the apartments. If I went to a strange house I'd be very lost. Here I have some neighbors in the house; I have relatives. But Bill and Sue don't seem to understand. They say, "You'll make friends." But the time to make friends is when your family is young, when your children are growing up. That's when you make friends, and those are the friends you keep.

When Rose and I finished talking, I asked her to sign a form giving me permission to use the taped material. She went next door to ask her neighbor, the nurse, to witness her signature. When her neighbor came into the apartment they hugged each other warmly, each saying how lucky she was to have the other as a neighbor.

CHAPTER 8

Marion DeLuca

During the Depression my mother was on home relief and when
we had to stand in line and wait for the clothes they would give
us or the measly food they were handing out, it was miserable . . .
But I've had it with that . . . As long as I have ten healthy fingers
and I'm well, I can always try to do something. I could make a
hem, do alterations, anything. If you want to do it, you can do it.

Marion DeLuca is a slim, fifty-eight-year-old woman. She has a
long, lined face; her short hair is fashionably cut and streaked; and although she speaks with a slight stutter that occasionally slows her
down, her manner is direct and un-self-conscious. When we first met,
she was wearing dark pants with a white turtleneck jersey, and two gold
chains—one of which bore the OA (Overeaters Anonymous) medallion,
and the other a gold mezuzah, a religious article of the Jewish faith that
contains a small folded or rolled parchment inscribed with scriptural
verses.

Marion and her husband live in a modern, six-story, red brick
building—one of several co-ops in the immediate area, which also includes semi-attached two-family houses, row houses, and five-story
walk-ups. The co-ops are clearly the most expensive housing in the
area. They are approximately twenty years old, and the entrance hall in
the DeLucas' building is immaculately clean and brightly lit. Near the
elevator are notices from the tenants' association and the local block association.

Her three-room apartment is very comfortably furnished with traditional furniture and elaborate draperies in both the living room and
the bedroom. A large color television set is in a central position in the
living room; needlepoint pictures that Marion has worked hang on the
walls; and a sewing machine that she uses to make many of her own
clothes is in the corner. The DeLucas' kitchen is bright and attractive.
Yellow and orange cabinets and copper-colored kitchen equipment
have been carefully coordinated with the brown, orange, white, and
gold modern print wallpaper.

The DeLucas married when Marion was in her late thirties. There
are no children from this marriage (Marion's first), although Frank
DeLuca has a son from a previous marriage. She works in a shop mak-

ing costumes, is a member of the International Ladies' Garment Workers Union, and earns $180.00 a week before taxes. Her husband was a die reamer at a company that went bankrupt. Because he lost his job as a result of the importing of steel, he is currently collecting unemployment insurance and fair trade readjustment allowances from the federal government. During our conversation Marion occasionally called her husband in to clarify or corroborate a point she was making; they seemed to function very much as a team.

We began by talking about problems in their apartment building and in their neighborhood.

Now, how can I express it? I am not against integration. In certain ways I am and in certain ways I'm not. I am on the board of my co-op and we have different nationalities and races in this building, but as long as I am screening I am screening for the best. We screen them financially. They have to have the money to come in; they have to buy their own apartments; they have to be able to keep up the rents. When they come in you can tell a person by the way they dress, the way they look, the way they talk. That's the only way; we can't go into their homes and screen them. And then we have a credit agency that screens out the rest. The majority right now is white, over ninety percent. But this past year we had a very big exodus. Mostly people who are retiring, people that have lived here since the building is up, their children are married now and they figured it's time to go. And we have a mixture of black, white, and Hispanic coming in.

I discriminate—I discriminate about cleanliness, about people just being human beings, about being a person not an animal, and this is what I have right now against New York. We have a bunch of animals living here. To me they are animals 'cause I travel with them on the subway and the majority of them have chips on their shoulders. How can I put it? Some of them never left the jungle. This is the only way I can put it. They have lived in the jungle all of their lives, some of them, and even though they are bettering themselves they are bettering themselves money-wise, but environment-wise they are not. They still live in the jungle in my opinion. They think that whatever is coming to them is coming to them because the world has kept them down for so long. Oh yes, I also discriminate when I hear young Hispanics talking in Spanish to one another. I grew up with a mother that understood very little English, and I can see a younger person conversing with an older person in their mother's tongue—I can understand that—but I can't see where children are going to school, and coming right out of school they go right back to their mother tongue. I can't see that. 'Cause English is my language. But, of course, as my organization OA has taught me, I can't change the world; I can only change myself.

It's a quiet area. According to the Police Department, we are a small crime area. Thank God for that. I've lived and been brought up in New York for fifty-eight years but I can't wait to get out. My husband wants to go south because his son is there, and I'm ready to go tomorrow. I retire in three-and-a-half years, so now I just take one day at a time.

I'm also on the board of the local block association. It's a civilian patrol. As you know, there are some people that are doers and some people that are sitters. I'm not a sitter. I get involved. I have to be involved in everything I get interested in.

We try to keep our area as best as we can. The volunteers go around in their own cars each night. Each one has their own hours, their own code name. If they see anything suspicious, they phone it in on the CB to the home office. Everybody has a CB in their car. Our block patrol has bought some and we connected one in each car. Our home office is the synagogue on the next street and that's where they call it. It's all on a volunteer basis. As a matter of fact we had a meeting last night and the head of our block patrol announced that on Sunday from eleven in the morning until she went to bed at twelve midnight, a little boy was missing and around two o'clock his parents started to get suspicious so they called it in. When she went to bed at twelve o'clock Sunday evening, she heard from the CB that the other civilian block patrols from all the areas came into this area looking for the child and they had a clue of where the child could be. I don't know if the child was found or not. So they do go on other things besides crime.

If, for instance, something is happening to an older person and they just can't get to any help, if they call in the block patrol they will be helped. Every member knows where the block patrol is. As a matter of fact we just passed out this newsletter to everybody in the area. We're having a Christmas party for all the children.

The association was formed about a year, a year-and-a-half ago, with the idea there was so much crime that we in our area should try and protect our own. You know, muggings, pocketbooks taken, stores being broken into, things like that. So this is why it was formed, for protection in the area. It was to help the police 'cause the police can't be everywhere at the same time. It's like a vigilante group, let's not kid ourselves. Each area has a vigilante group.

Of course, the block patrol cannot get out of their car to help anybody. They have to call in to the home office to get help, and the home office calls in to the police. The people who started the association are people who have been living in the area a long time. We felt we can help our area, keep it as safe as it is. I really don't know if it makes a difference, but when I come home at night I feel a little bit more comfortable. At one time you were able to walk in New York at eight o'clock at night; I don't feel safe walking at eight o'clock anymore. But at least I know that there's a car going around. It may not be in the area just where I am at that particular moment, but I do know that there's a car going around. But if we don't get more volunteers we may have to fold.

It's not just this area, it's all of New York. We've had incidents in the daytime. One woman was mugged twice in the daytime right here on this block. Another woman's bag was snatched. When I'm not working and I have to come home from Manhattan at twelve o'clock in the afternoon, I will not ride the subway; I'll take the express bus. I take the subway in the morning to go to work and to come home, but that's the only time. I am fearful of my life. I have never been that way before. Look, I give this area tops three years; it's going to turn. Under me is a Spanish couple, a middle-aged couple—they ran away. They were robbed three times, lovely people. I made friends out of them, very lovely people. So I don't discriminate, as I said before, against race or religion or the person; I discriminate against animals.

Marion DeLuca continued by talking about her childhood, her humiliation at being on welfare (then known as "home relief"), and her family's struggle to get out of the ghetto and achieve a comfortable life. She related her current views to her early experiences and essentially posed the question: If we managed to survive through hard work and at least partial assimilation, why can't they today?

I was born on the Lower East Side. I'm a product of the Lower East Side. When I was six years old we moved to the Bronx. My mother and father came from Russia. They were distantly related and it was not a happy marriage. Sorry to say, but it wasn't, so it was better that they were separated. We were eight children; we're now four. There were two that I never knew and the other two that passed on I knew, but they were much older. I was the next-to-the-youngest.

My parents separated, I think, when I was at the age of around twelve or thirteen. He moved in, he moved out, he moved in, he moved out, but the last separation was it.

My mother never worked. She couldn't. She had enough kids to take care of, so how could she work? But we always lived on a day-to-day basis. We managed. There was plenty of love in the house so we managed. And what can I tell you? She always had respect for my father. She—how could I say that she loved him, to her stroke day, to her dying day. And when he died I just felt I didn't want to sit Shiva* so she said to me I have to because of respect that I carry his name. Even when she was dying, she kept asking for my father. We knew she always cared for him. That was her life. It was a misfortune, but it was her life. I see now that he was in AA.** Too bad that we couldn't help him then.

During the Depression my mother was on home relief and when we had to stand in line and wait for the clothes they

---

* The Jewish period of mourning.
** Alcoholics Anonymous.

would give us or the measly food they were handing out, it was miserable, but I had to stand and receive it for my mother. But I've had it with that. That's why I can't see somebody standing around on the corner and I have to pay for it. When they wait for their relief checks, my taxes have to pay for it. We were there out of circumstances. When we went on relief we had WPA,* we had the NRA,** but we were there out of circumstances, not out of choice. But today a lot of these welfare cases are out of choice. Oh yes, a lot of them are. And how many are stealing from the welfare out of choice? Yes, I do resent them.

If they're unable, then a country like ours should give. Nobody in our country should go hungry, nobody. We have elderly that need help, that's beautiful. We have young people that need help, fine. But I can't see where somebody's standing on the street corner just waiting for welfare because of their ethnic group. They are using their deprived status over the years to get what's coming to them. That's my opinion, mine and a lot more like me. 'Cause I also know what poorness is and was, but that didn't stop me. I also had a job, I also started to work for eight dollars a week, fifty-two hours in the week. Nothing was handed to me on a platter. We had to work for what we have, so I know what work means. So, I do resent them.

Yes, I think there are jobs out there—any kind of job. There is nothing wrong with washing somebody else's floor, an honest living. I have a brother, thank God he doesn't have to, but he once made the statement, "If I have to wash somebody else's floor, a dollar I will always earn." 'Cause he also is a child of circumstances. He was also brought up by people donating things and he swore he will never go through it again. He can wash floors, do windows—he'll always earn a dollar, and that's the way I see it. As long as I have ten healthy fingers and I'm

---

* Work Projects Administration—A public works program established in 1936 to provide jobs instead of direct relief payments for the unemployed during the Depression.

** National Recovery Administration—A US government agency established in 1933 to stimulate business recovery during the Depression through fair practice codes which aimed at eliminating unfair trade practices, reducing unemployment, establishing minimum wages and maximum hours, and guaranteeing the right of labor to bargain collectively.

well, I can always try to do something. I could make a hem, do alterations, anything. If you want to do it, you can do it. As I said, if they're not able to, that's another story. But why should we just hand out the money? I work too hard for it to hand it out that way.

My parents came from Europe, but they worked hard. A lot of people came out of ghettos from down on the Lower East Side. We made our own ghetto, too, because we lived in the circle where our parents were able to talk the language. We struggled and a lot of them learned the language and came out of the ghetto to give their children a better education. My mother spoke Yiddish, but we didn't speak Yiddish. I spoke English to my friends. I spoke to my mother in half-and-half. I know when I went to school we had our report card in English. My mother didn't have it in Yiddish or in Hebrew. That's what I resent. I resent it fiercely. This is my country, not their country. This is their country? Fine. You want to make it your country? That's beautiful. We are a real big country, but come do things like we do. We took up the way of this country. We came to better ourselves, not to have the country come down to our level.

Roosevelt? I loved him. That was my first president that I voted for and I felt he was our king, he was our everything. Of course times were bad but I think he did wonders for us. I saw him when he made the trip to all the boroughs of New York City and I was thrilled. I felt he was a working man's dream. I always have to consider myself in the working class; I'm nothing else but—that's why I have a soft heart for the union.

We were strictly Democrats right down the line. To this very day. Carter? I voted for him as there was nobody else to vote for, but I don't think he's the best man that could have been put up by the Democrats. But another Roosevelt we can't have. I sort of liked Jack Kennedy but not Robert Kennedy. I feel that Jack Kennedy, we don't know what he would have done because he was cut too short in life. I liked the man. Ted Kennedy—I can't see him as president either. I felt right now it's got to be Jimmy Carter because I couldn't see a Republican president; we've had enough of them. And whenever we've had them I think the working man was put right down the drain.

As I said, we'll never have another Roosevelt. And I'll tell you a little secret, we'll never have another Truman. I liked him because he didn't give a good damn who was around, he just came right out and told you the way he felt. That's why I liked him. He was a straightforward man. As far as I can see he was good for the working man, to the working class and the middle class, but today we have no middle class. One time we had three classes—rich, middle, and poor. But today we have four classes—rich, upper middle, lower middle, and poor.

If you're making thirty-five thousand now, you're considered middle class, but upper middle class. Some middle classes make ten thousand; that's like being poor, but they still consider you in the middle class. I'm poor middle class, believe me I am. At one time I was just considered middle class but not today anymore. We don't earn as much as the upper middle class. Because a man is in a profession doesn't put him into the wealthy class. It's by money, strictly by money, not the person himself. The person himself has nothing to do with it. The person is a human being. And you know yourself, if a man and a wife aren't working, you can't live today. Unless you want to live as a poor class, get subsidy and get help.

What should the government do to help people? I believe that the government should take over the medical plans of the people—just like in England—but I know it will never be. Not in my time. It may be in somebody else's time, but not in my time. The AMA* will not allow it. How will they become millionaires? At one time your doctor made a house call. Now if you call him for an emergency he makes an appointment with you. You could be dying now, but the appointment has to be made for next week. One time I didn't feel this way, but now I do. The doctors themselves made me feel that I want national health service. You have a bellyache, so instead of going to the

* American Medical Association.

general practitioner he sends you to the stomach specialist. Everybody's become a specialist in their own field, and you pay for it. You pay right through the nose.

Marion talked about her relationship with her mother, the years they lived together after she was married, and her mother's final illness.

Frankie, how long is Momma dead? January this year will be fourteen years. But actually I would say she was dead two-and-a-half years before that because she had a stroke and after the stroke she knew nothing anymore. Then she was in a home. We couldn't take care of her. Impossible. She was dead weight and she knew nothing. Lost control of herself and everything else. But she died at the age of eighty-two. Lived a beautiful life. Played cards till four, five in the morning. As a matter of fact, the day of her stroke a friend came up to play some rummy in the house, and she had the stroke right in front of my eyes. We were sitting together in the living room and she went right off.

I lived at home with my mother until I got married at thirty-eight. We've been married twenty years. This is my husband's second marriage; it's the first for me. I married late but no regrets. It's a good marriage. Different religions but it's a good marriage. My mother used to say at the beginning that he was a Spanish Jew, but after a while if anybody asked her who her favorite son-in-law was, it was him.

When we got married my mother lived with us, and my sisters and brother gave my mother money for herself. Not for the house because my husband didn't allow it, just for herself so she could be independent in buying her own things. When she had to do a little bit of shopping and I wanted to give her money, she said, "Oh, no."

When we got married my husband moved in with us into a one-bedroom apartment. Then we got a two-bedroom apartment and then she says, "Well, now we're going to the bigger place and I'm going to live with my daughter." You know, she made the transition. She was not a stupid woman. She was never in our way; it worked very well, even with the TV. They both liked cowboy things. I still say you cannot find children today like the children of yesterday. Children were independent in my time, too, but in a different way. I always say I was good, after thirty-eight years still living with my mother. I always wanted my own place but I always felt a little guilt about leaving her alone. Children of today don't feel that way. They reach an age where they're working—out they go. I don't know who's the better off, they or I.

When she was a little younger she might have been able to live alone if she could have supported herself, but she couldn't. Let's see, how can I put it? She had to live on our income. Then when she was later on in years I wouldn't have left her because at one time she had a coronary thrombosis which didn't kill her, but she had it—and she had a breast removed. And, as my mother would always say, when she went to bed at night she became half a person because she would have to take her hearing aid off, she would have to take her glasses off, her teeth would have to come out of her mouth, and her breast would have to come off. When she got up in the morning she became a whole person again. But she lived through it all and functioned very well. When she walked out of the house she always had her little powder and toilet water on and she always had a hat on. She had to show her daughter's trade.

Marion described her work, in which she obviously takes considerable pride. She is, however, critical of the seniority system in her union as well as the pressures of piecework, and she emphasizes the cooperative way in which she and a small group of co-workers work in spite of union policy and the policy of the majority of workers in her shop. She clearly feels ambivalent about the role of unions, but on balance thinks "it would be worse without one."

I work in mid-Manhattan at a place that makes costumes. Near where all the pimps, hookers, and real derelicts hang out. When I walk by, I walk with my head down; I don't walk, I run. Usually when we go home from there we go home in groups of threes, so it's not bad, you know. I'm working at this company—it will be two years in June. I make the headpieces for the costumes. Prior to that I had been a milliner. I worked in women's millinery since 1937 and I gave it up two years ago. I changed because I was getting ill working in the place I was in, and millinery is a dying industry, a real dying industry. Right now, women are not wearing hats.

I worked for two firms in all my years of working. I'm a copier. I started out as a floor-girl and worked my way into becoming a pieceworker. If the hat's made from a frame, they would give you the frame and you would cover the frame and set it up and do all the rest to make it into a hat. I did it all; I made the whole hat. I did like my work. I still do. I like to see a finished product. But now I'm not doing piecework anymore. Now, I'm strictly "week work"—I get a weekly salary.

We made not only the headpieces, but all the costumes for *Roots* on TV. We made them for *Sesame Street, Captain Kangaroo*—for a lot of the TV shows. It's one of the biggest costume companies in New York. Thursday, in the Thanksgiving Day parade, the Rockettes are wearing the hats that I made. I started from scratch. The frame work, the putting on of the felt, and all. We work as a group, as a whole individual group. Sometimes I'll start on a piece of work and something else will come in, so it's dropped. So if somebody else needs work they will pick it up and continue on. We are one, two—actually we are four girls. The supervisor and three others. We just got through working on the movie of *The Wiz*. We made all the headpieces. If you see it, you will know that Emerald City was made at the shop where I work.

It's a big costume place—part of the Dressmakers' Union, Local 22. It's a funny sort of a union because the older people don't want the younger ones to come in. It's seniority they work by and it's a bad system, but that's the way they've kept it all these years. To step ahead you have to wait for somebody to retire or for somebody to die; that's the whole crux of it. And these oldsters don't want to retire. We have a man that's in his eighties who is still working.

I think in my shop alone if we have five people in their fifties they're considered young. I think it's wrong. I think that there shouldn't be seniority. I think it should be that once you become a member of the shop you should be considered as a member of the shop and share time with people. You work a month and I work a month. That's what we do in millinery. But the other parts of the shop, they work by seniority. The minute it gets slow they will lay you off if you haven't got seniority. The senior member can stay; they can work fifty-two weeks of the year while you don't. In our department we girls have decided that we'd like some time off in between so we have decided that we are going to share time when it gets slow. In a regular millinery firm they share time; they always did. So because I work with an ex-milliner and with an ex-operator from lingerie who also shared time, we have decided that when it gets slow each one will work and each one will have some time off.

What do I think of the union? It would be worse without a union. I'm a strong union person. I have to be because I'm a working person. But we all know what unions are. Let's not kid ourselves. We know sometimes that they play with the bosses. They give in to the workers on certain issues, but I feel in my heart they give in more to the bosses than they do to the workers. And we know that they are trying to take over, but it has to be. As I said before, it would be worse without a union. If a boss didn't like you, well, look, he could kick you out, you know that. So we need the union, the worker needs the union. I have been in a union all my life.

I started to work when I was sixteen going on seventeen and I'm fifty-eight now. I went to trade school for millinery and I stayed in the trade that I had taken up. I wanted to be a nurse, but finances did not let me. I couldn't afford to go through high school and I couldn't afford to go through nursing school, 'cause I was in the Depression and I knew that I had to learn a trade to be able to keep myself. I finished my two years of trade school and went right to work.

In addition to her block association and tenants' association, Marion DeLuca belongs to yet another self-help group, Overeaters Anonymous. The self-help movement has developed rapidly since the late 1960s, focusing particularly on issues of safety, neighborhood preservation, and medical care. It has been estimated that there are currently over a half-million different self-help groups in this country; some of the most successful deal with various forms of addiction (Gamblers Anonymous, Alcoholics Anonymous, groups formed to combat the use of other drugs, Overeaters Anonymous, and Weight Watchers). These groups have often succeeded in helping people when all other methods have failed. Marion described what Overeaters Anonymous has meant to her, not only in enabling her to maintain a reasonable weight, but in other areas of her life as well.

I was heavy all my life, and like a heavy person you go on all different diets. At the age of twelve and thirteen I was two hundred pounds, and this is the way I grew up. I went from one doctor to another—pills, clinics, Weight Watchers, until finally I hit OA. I knew about OA through my sister-in-law's sister but I didn't want to go into it because I thought they were kooks. But I knew finally I had to hit it and I did it. And I love it. It has changed my life. I didn't lose a tremendous amount of weight, but I tried to straighten out my head which is where I know it stems from more than anything else. I've changed some of my life but I've still got a long way to go.

We have twelve steps and twelve traditions and this is the way I live now. I live my OA teachings. Not only in my eating habits but in my way of life. I take one day at a time. I do not worry about yesterday, 'cause whatever happened happened yesterday and I cannot change it. I don't worry about tomorrow, 'cause my tomorrows never come. I don't worry about today either 'cause when I get up in the morning I throw my life out to God and I'm in God's hands for the day. OA has taught me that. OA has taught me to give up my resentments, as they say. I can't say I love my father, I can't say I respected him, but I have learned now that my father was ill and I have to give up all the resentments. So if I can't say anything good I'll just say, "Rest in Peace." I'm trying, trying, trying every day to take an inventory of my own life, of my own self, to see where and how I have failed and to try to better myself as I go on now. This is all OA teaching.

In February of '78 I will have been in OA three years and I have maintained my weight for two-and-a-half years. And I just love it. I do as much as I can for OA 'cause it has given me a new lease on life. I am an overeater. I will always be a compulsive overeater. There are certain foods that I wouldn't even dare to put into my mouth 'cause one bite is not enough for me—but I can live, I can breathe, I can do things. If I could go out in the world and see every heavy person, I would run and tell them that there's help for them in the world. They should not despair, but they've got to want it. They've got to want it as bad as I want it. It's just a beautiful organization. If you want it bad enough, you'll find what you want in OA. Since I've joined OA my feelings about myself have changed. I am not a worrier anymore.

My husband is out of work now a little over a year. His firm has given up after thirty-three years in business. He worked there as a die reamer for thirty-three years. He had a nice job, beautiful benefits, but he lost it when the company went out of business and then it was bought by a black outfit and subsidized by the government. Now the policy is to hire one black, one Hispanic, one white. He sent in a résumé in the hope that they may need him. Right now he is still collecting unemployment and fair trade readjustment allowances. The government is subsidizing him for a year and a half because he lost his job due to imported steel.

When he reaches seventy-eight payments, that will be around March of next year, then he'll look for work. It doesn't really pay for him to look for work now, you know, 'cause he wouldn't get anywhere near the money he's getting. But if the company ever called him, he'd go back to work right now. We had plans where he'd work till sixty-five, but unfortunately . . .

He does get itchy being at home but he keeps busy. He does the laundry, the house cleaning, the vacuuming. Even when we both worked, we worked together. He would do the laundry for me in the morning and the dusting and all that; it helps. I'm sure he'll find a job. I have no problems. See, that's what I'm trying to tell you. At one time I was a worry-bird, I would worry about it. I would worry my husband is out of work. But now God has taken it away from me.

I always knew we had a God above us but I always questioned God. I questioned God for my mother's life—I questioned God why He had to take four children from her, why she had to live such a, well, to me it was a miserable life: no money, no love, no help. But I shouldn't say that either, because she had love from her children, she had love from her brother, she had love from her sister and brother-in-law, but she had no husband beside her. He was always there to make a baby but he was never there to take care of it. And I would question it. I would ask her and she always would answer me, "We don't question, we have to accept what God has given us."

To me God was a bargaining God. I used to say to Him, "If you do this for me I'll do this for you." But since OA I found out that you don't bargain with God because God is there and God will answer you. But also God tells me that if I don't help myself He can't help me. My belief in God now is a different belief than what I had as a child when growing up. The belief I had in God before was a fearful God, a God who punished. God doesn't punish. God is there. He's there to help everybody—me, you, the derelict, and everybody else.

I still go to my maintenance meetings which I won't give up and I've started now a fourth-step meeting which is a personal inventory of myself; just this past Sunday we had a Marathon, an all-day session. I attend because I feel it helps me. Everytime I say to my husband, "I'm not going to go this week." But I go. It helps me become a better person. As we say in OA, "It's my shot in my arm." It helps me to go on.

At meetings I share and I give. I give as much as I can of myself, 'cause I have found a beautiful way of life and I try to give it to others, I try to teach them what I have learned. I'm trying to give them what I have found in my spiritual life. Everybody that joins OA is there on their own. Nobody is compelled. The meetings are run by everybody. We do have a leader and a qualifier for the evening but OA is run by everybody, not by one person.

OA is a self-help group of people who are all compulsive overeaters. We are not connected with AA but we use their literature, their philosophy, their twelve steps and twelve traditions. Today they have recognized alcoholism as a sickness and in due time they are going to recognize overeating as a sickness, too. I think it started on the West Coast, but it's all over the world now. We even have meetings in Israel. Men and women, teenagers, anybody who is willing to say, "Hey, I'm a compulsive overeater, help me"—we are there to help them. You get up and you introduce yourself by your first name only and you're welcomed into the crowd. Anybody can get up and talk. You just give what you feel on the inside. If you're good, bad, or indifferent, this is where you let it out. We hope with our anonymity it stays within the room. That's why we call it Overeaters Anonymous. It's a beautiful organization.

If it wasn't for OA I would never have changed my job. I had worked in the job I had prior to this one practically all my life, and toward the end of it I was getting sick of it. I would come home every night and drive Frankie insane. I couldn't take the bickering, I couldn't take the politiking going on there. It was all politics. When you're a pieceworker, you're greedy, let's not kid ourselves. Every pieceworker is greedy in a way 'cause if you're not you're not going to make out for the day, and you're working to make out. And when you had a little argument with the forelady and you saw your good work given away to somebody else, and you had to keep asking, "I need work, I need work," it started to eat me. And I saw what was going on there in the shop and I couldn't take it because I'm a person where—let me live; I let you live—but share with me. I would come home and drive him insane. Then my present job came up through my millinery union and I was given the decision of which job do I want?

How did OA help me make my decision? It has helped me to grow. I knew that whatever I was deciding that God was deciding with me. I know that I am a better person and that I could do the job. I have much more confidence in myself. I still have a long way to go to get some more confidence, 'cause there are times when they give me something to do and I say to myself, "God help me, can I do it?" This job is more of a challenge and it's healthier for me. At least I know when I go to work in the morning, I'm getting paid for my day's work. I don't have to fight to earn my money. And it's a more peaceful and restful job. I earn a hundred and eighty dollars gross for a thirty-five-hour week.

When you come into OA you're new; you're a baby; you

have to take on a sponsor, who is a guide, nothing else but a guide through the program. We have a saying, "Before you take your first bite, phone. Call somebody. Call for help." You can call anybody in OA. If you want to call your sponsor, you call your sponsor. If you don't want to call your sponsor, you call somebody else, but before you take that first bite, call, 'cause that person, if they're really into it, they're going to give you help.

I love sponsoring a maintenance person. I haven't sponsored a baby in over a year. Just three months ago somebody came and said, "Take this baby on." It was a young man. I was skeptical but I took him. Two weeks it didn't work, then all of a sudden, I have to use a little slang, I said to him, "Look, boy, either you shit or you get off this pot. I can't bicker with you any more." And finally he came through with flying colors. He is such an OA-er that it is really amazing. He has lost beautifully, he has picked up the program beautifully.

In OA I have learned one thing—that's discipline in eating habits. I live on three meals a day with nothing in between, except diet soda, coffee, or sugarless chewing gum. If I will have a binge, I'll have a binge at mealtime. At least I have learned through OA to have just one meal at a time. At the beginning I used to find it hard saying, "One day at a time." Later on I had to live from one hour at a time, 'cause as you get into it, it gets a little harder. And now there are days I find it rough, there are days I find it like a breeze. But I don't only belong to OA; I have an OA husband. He goes along with me beautifully. I drive, but I do not like to drive alone at night 'cause even if I take the car, he has to come down to go into the garage with me, so it's easier for him to drive me to OA. At the beginning he came to a few meetings. Now he doesn't. Everybody in OA knows my husband. We work together in everything.

I always say, and they laugh at me at my meetings, but I always say, "I haven't got one higher power, I have two higher powers working for me. I have Moses on my right shoulder and I have Christ on my left shoulder." All religion is kept in my house. We belong to the temple and, as a matter of fact, we have more Jewish friends than we have non-Jewish friends. When we got married, his older sister tried to convert me and my oldest brother-in-law tried to convert him, and I told them plain up and down that we married each other for what we are, so don't try to convert us. We are staying as we are. But one thing I say: we are living together, we're going to lay together in death, too. I made him join the Oddfellows because of burial purposes only, so we can be together. Nobody knows whose tomorrow it is and I don't want his family to come and say he's a Catholic or my family to say I'm Jewish. If we're good enough to live together, we're good enough to be beside one another. As he would say, I'm going to nudge him in death, too.

Women's lib? I always had women's lib. I was always a free woman, but I still like to be treated as a woman by a man. I don't want to give up my privilege of being a woman. I am not a man's equal, no. I don't believe in that. I believe in women's lib where they should have equal jobs—the one who is entitled to it should have it, yes. Don't outdo me because you're a man when I can either do a better job or just as equal as you. But I still want the privilege where a man will respect me and say, "Hey, she's a woman."

I am not opposed to abortions; no, I say they should have it. Nobody can tell me what to do with my own body. No person has the right to tell me when to have my child and when not to have my child. Yes, I believe in the right of abortion.

Yes, I share my housework. I believe that marriage should be a fifty-fifty basis, not just one way. Even though, when I am home, I try to do a little more than he does but it doesn't work that way. He's like I am. I sit and sew, I make my own clothes, and when I sew, he'll put up half the supper. We do things on an equal basis.

No, I have no children of my own. I felt if I couldn't grow up young with my children—I felt that by the time I would reach the age of sixty I could have a child of twenty, where's the contrast? When my little grandnieces come to me, I love every one of them, but I can't wait for them to go home. I like the peace and quiet of my home. So I see now that in a way it was good not to have any children, 'cause I don't think I'd be able to take a child now constantly with me.

Yet I regret not having a child 'cause I love children. We both love children. But when we got married we didn't have anything. We couldn't even afford to make our own wedding. All we had was twenty fingers between us. We really had to work for whatever we have. And whatever we have—our home, our car, our savings—whatever we have, he and I did together. We had to support my husband's son. He's a lawyer now; he's married and now his wife is going to law school, too. I'm not a millionaire; I can't say we're overabundant, comfortable people, but whatever we have we're satisfied. I have a car, I have my home, and I'm looking forward to retirement. And what's more, we are both healthy people. Really, what more is there in life?

Reflections

As we come marching, marching, we bring the greater days.
The rising of the women means the rising of the race.
No more the drudge and idler—ten that toil where one reposes,
But a sharing of life's glories: Bread and roses! Bread and roses!
—James Oppenheimer

We have glimpsed the lives of eight women. None of them are famous—they are not the superstars of our society—but they have much to teach us. None are avid feminists but neither do they disagree so very much with the women's movement. None are particularly preoccupied with political problems but all of them see the larger ramifications of issues that touch them closely. Perhaps most important, none are two-dimensional cardboard figures, as working-class people are so often portrayed in our society.

Each of these women has a perspective developed out of her particular family history, her racial, religious and ethnic background, and her concrete life experience. How do they feel, for example, about their role as women in our society? Diane DiMarco stresses the dominant role of men in her life: her brother was abusive to her when they lived together even when she was paying the bills; a former fiancé refused to permit her to enter the occupation she preferred and instead helped her to obtain her present job, about which she is at the very least ambivalent; another male friend was primarily responsible for her use of drugs and for her only criminal escapade; and when she has been in trouble, men have also, as she says, "straightened her out." She feels that her only hope now for a better life lies with her father's release from prison. Diane presents herself as one who is acted upon by the male world around her.

Christina Ramos, on the other hand, sees herself as an independent woman who has refused to stay with her husband "for better or for worse." "For worse," she says, she would rather be by herself. Consequently, she is making her way alone with her daughter, trying to make some sense out of the world around her, even though she acknowledges that it is, at times, a difficult and lonely way to live.

And then there are those women who are trying to make a life with a man and yet at the same time have an independent life of their own:

Marion DeLuca, who married in her late thirties and has since maintained a wide variety of activities, and Maria Perez who is attempting to balance part-time work, a commitment to an extended family, the raising of three children, and a marital relationship.

Some of the women frankly admit that they are holding back, that to some extent they are submerging their needs and talents for the sake of their husbands or their families: Elinor Thomas, who is sacrificing her desire to work because of her husband's objections, states, "I feel, to be truthful, that I'm keeping myself down, that I am the strongest one. In a sense I feel my husband looks up to me, but somehow or another, I try to tone that down and make him stay up there, you know, because I feel that's the way it should be." Frances Meyers talks somewhat sadly about how she "submerged" herself in her husband's life for years, protecting and shielding him, and says that one of the reasons she did not return to bookkeeping was because she thought that "if I made more money than he did it would degrade him."

And yet while their relationship to their work is often determined, at least in part, by their family relationships, work plays a central role in these women's lives. Forty-two percent of American women were employed in 1975—thirty-one percent in full-time jobs and eleven percent in part-time jobs.[1] Because the women I interviewed are working-class people for whom work is often an economic necessity, a far higher percentage of them work outside their homes than do women in the total population: of the eight women, seven have outside jobs—six full-time and one part-time. All work in overwhelmingly female occupations. Diane is a typist; ninety-seven percent of all typists in the United States in 1975 were women. Rose is a waitress; ninety-one percent of all those waiting on tables in restaurants in 1975 were female. Marion is a milliner; ninety-six percent of all stitchers and sewers in 1975 were women. Maria is a ward secretary in a hospital, and when Elinor worked outside of her home she was a nurse's aide; eighty-six percent of all nurse's aides in 1975 were female.[2]

Occupational sex-typing—that is, women working predominantly for low pay in service, sales, and clerical jobs—has been a major factor in the widening gap between the earnings of men and women during the past ten years. In 1967 the median annual income of women was slightly over $4,000 and the median annual income of men was just under $8,000, a difference of approximately $4,000; in 1976 the median annual income for women was $8,000 and for men it was just under $14,000, a difference of approximately $6,000 per year.[3] Furthermore, the median income of the twenty-five percent of American households "headed" by a female in 1976 was $5,760 compared to a median income of $15,300 in those "headed" by a male.[4] Occupational sex-typing, low wages, and limited job mobility severely limit women's choices, not only in the sphere of work, but also within their private lives—in their marital arrangements, their childrearing patterns, and their view of themselves.

But the choice of whether or not to work is not a luxury these women can afford: Diane, Christina, Frances, and Rose must support themselves; Gwen must work if she is to have any flexibility within her marriage; Maria claims her family must have two incomes in order to pay their bills; and Marion's job is all the more essential since her husband has been laid off and his work future is uncertain. Even Elinor, who is not working, is, in reality, earning needed added income by caring for a foster child.

While work is an economic necessity, it is often a source of self-esteem as well: Elinor Thomas says, "When I was working, I was bringing in something like $160 every two weeks and, you know, you feel so good to be able to do a lot of things that we could not do before. And I wasn't being selfish; it wasn't like my money. It was to be shared by everyone." Gwen Johnson states, "I was making a hundred dollars for the first time in my life and so I was just happy, you know. I really got involved—in welfare issues, rent strikes, food co-ops. It got me out of the house, out of my rut." Rose O'Rourke says, "Mike used to often say to me, 'Why don't you stay home, Rose ... you don't have to work.' I used to say to him, 'I enjoy it, Mike.' The couple of hours mean so much to me and the extra money was nice, too. And I loved it. I love to get out."

But as Eli Zaretsky has observed in his analysis of the relationship between capitalist society and the family, "... even working women give the family their primary allegiance."[5] In spite of their work many of these women think that a woman's first responsibility is caring for the home and the children particularly when the children are young. They also think, however, that once their responsibilities at home are met, outside work can add an important dimension to their lives. Perhaps Frances Meyers states this point of view most forcefully: "I don't see how any woman with any ounce of brains could stay in the house continuously unless she does something to occupy her time. Any woman who just stays in, cooks, and cleans ... it becomes very dull. There's nothing to learn, nothing to see, no one to speak to and compare different topics." Nevertheless, while they feel that the home should be a woman's first priority, several state that men ought to help around the house and the older women, particularly, describe the ways in which their husbands have shared extensively in the housework.

Work is seen both as a financial necessity and as a means of personal gratification to all of these women, including Elinor, but its frustrating, monotonous, alienating aspects are also discussed. Diane talks about the mindless quality of much of the routine clerical work she does; her satisfaction comes entirely from her social contacts at work. Marion talks about the cut-throat quality of doing piecework in the garment industry; and Frances discusses the reality of job insecurity and how this leads members of different ethnic groups to fight among themselves for the few available jobs.

While several of the women are members of trade unions, and all who discussed unions agreed that they were important because they protect your job, none of them spontaneously referred to the union as a possible vehicle for humanizing their work situation. Diane points out that unions protect women to some extent from sexual harassment and from being fired if they reject sexual advances; Rose, who is a waitress, feels mildly positive at best about her union; but Marion sums up their view when she says, "It would be worse without a union. I'm a strong union person. I have to be because I'm a working person. But we all know what unions are. Let's not kid ourselves ... If a boss didn't like you ... he could kick you out ... So we need the union, the worker needs the union."

For these women perhaps the most discouraging and debilitating experience has been the wasted effort of being trained, usually in federally funded programs, to work at jobs which were available at one time but are now no longer funded. According to Frances Fox Piven and Richard A. Cloward, the chief function of relief programs in this country, as in many other Western societies, is to "regulate the poor," to "absorb and control" unemployed people when "mass unemployment leads to outbreaks of turmoil" and then, "as turbulence subsides," to contract the programs and cast the marginal relief population back on the surplus labor market.[6] Their analysis of the Great Society's antipoverty programs in the 1960s indicates that a combination of forces— the pressure of black migration to northern cities, the traditional alliance between blacks and the Democratic party, and the escalating protests, demonstrations, and riots of the mid-1960s—led to direct intervention by the federal government, which established new services to give the poor, particularly poor urban blacks, increased access to the welfare system. Local programs were initiated that cultivated and trained "community workers." (In some ways this was a new form of ward politics and political patronage.) [7] When the turbulence of the 1960s diminished, the programs were constricted and the community workers were left without jobs.

Thus Gwen, who was trained by Mobilization for Youth to be a community worker, cannot find a job in New York City, and Christina, who has completed two years of college and has been trained by Teacher Corps to be a school aide, has lost her job because of funding cutbacks and has been unable to find another one. The anger these women feel has nowhere to go. Whom can they blame? To whom can they complain? They must try continually to reaffirm their own worth without external proof, for if working enhances other women's self-esteem, what does being unemployed for an extended period of time do to these women? Who is to say that an individual has value as a community worker or even as a person if she cannot get a job? How can she be sure it's the fault of the system and not her own? And, of course, it is no accident that one of these jobless women is black and the other is Hispanic, for the unemployment rate among blacks was over thirteen percent at the end of 1977—over twice the rate for whites[8]—and the rate of unemployment among Puerto Ricans living in the United States is at least twice the national rate.[9]

Unemployment statistics, however, are only one measure, albeit a critical one, of the oppression of blacks in our society. The median income of white households in 1976 was $13,290 and the median income of black households was $7,900.[10] Furthermore, while blacks constitute 10.8 percent of the total work force, they make up 26.3 percent of the blue collar, clerical, and sales workers in the United States and only 7.5 percent of the white collar workers, 4.5 percent of the managers and administrators, and 8.3 percent of the professional and technical workers.[11]

Elinor Thomas, perhaps the mildest and most conciliatory of all the women, clearly states the employment reality for many blacks: "... you always have a feeling that you're not going to be able to earn but so much, you know. I think this is the feeling in a lot of black people's minds, especially the head of the family, even my husband." She gives an example of why she and her husband feel this sense of futility—the promotion of a less-qualified worker to a supervisory position in the post office instead of Mr. Thomas. She explains further: "Yes, this person was white; it was a woman."

Perhaps one of the reasons that black women do not feel a greater solidarity with the women's movement is that they know that the most crucial issues for them are race and class, not sex—that whites, both men and women, will continue to be promoted over blacks and that their own status is not going to change significantly until racism is no longer a major factor in American life. As Elinor's husband explains to her: "You're not going to get but so high. Some people do but you've got to be . . . damn good if you get there. And then when you get there, if you're black, you've got to shine."

Class issues appear to be dividing blacks increasingly as those with education and technological skills are able to move more easily than in the past into corporate and government sectors of the economy while the poor are falling further behind. As one sociologist has recently noted, "A history of discrimination and oppression created a huge black underclass, and the technological and economic revolutions threaten to solidify its position in society." [12]

The economic situation for Puerto Ricans is no better. According to a recent article in the *New York Times:*

> Puerto Ricans are at the bottom of the economic ladder, worse off than other Hispanics and most other ethnic groups. Their population is three times poorer than the national average. One of every four families depends on welfare, entirely or in part . . . Even with their ability to speak English and urban education, second and third generation Puerto Ricans have not done much better than their elders. Gains made in the 1960's have eroded; the percentage of those living in poverty rose from 29 percent in 1970 to 33 percent in 1974, and may have risen further since then. [13]

If the economic situation of so many black and Puerto Rican families is this desperate, do these women feel that human-service institutions are helping to ease the poverty or despair of minority people? The human-service sector, enormously complex and chaotic, includes federally funded services, state-funded services, city-funded services, and nongovernmentally funded services (both profit-making and non–profit-making). Many overlap in function and in population served. At the same time, particularly in recent years with significant financial cutbacks at all levels, huge gaps exist in the services provided and many groups of people are ineligible to receive the services that do exist. Varying eligibility requirements make the picture even more incomprehensible to the consumer (and often to the professional social worker as well) and the required income threshold is so low that it excludes much of the working class.

Gwen, who has had considerable experience with human services both as a consumer and as a provider, vehemently states that programs for blacks and for the poor are instituted primarily as a method of social control and as a means of helping white, middle-class people. She goes on to discuss the use of methadone to treat heroin addiction and the reasons she sees for this form of treatment: "Just like the addict. They tell him if you get on the methadone program, you're going to be better but you're not. Their agenda is not that you're going to be better for yourself, but . . . you're not going to be hitting anybody in the head, robbing them, and that's why methadone was given to most of the addicts . . . not to make them viable human beings, but to protect society."

Gwen describes vividly what is often termed the "medicalization" of the treatment of drug addiction and its use as a form of social control. The medical-care system has increasingly enveloped many aspects of people's daily lives, aspects that were once managed by the individual, the nuclear family, the extended family, friends, neighbors, or others in the community. In addition to this outreach into the realm of problems that were formerly considered "personal" (methods of parenting, problems with sex, and the anguish of death and dying, for example), the medical system has also begun to concern itself with issues that were once seen as legal or moral. Medical expropriation of the areas of drug abuse, alcoholism, and child abuse has in recent years caused the medical-care system increasingly to become an institution of social control.[14] While medicalization of behavior deemed deviant by the society has been accompanied by, and to some extent caused by, the decriminalization of that behavior, at least in the middle class, the question remains whether this medical treatment is any less repressive, any less punitive, than former sanctions. Is medicalization simply a "civilized" society's way of "managing" unpleasant behavior?

Gwen claims that the medicalization of drug abuse did not take place until "it became a middle class, white problem, then it became something to look out for, something to get statistics on, something to set up programs for 'cause you weren't going to send *them* to jail. You're not going to put *their* kids in jail."

The two-class character of American medical care (one system for the middle class and the affluent, another for the poor and the working class) was emphasized over and over by the women whom I interviewed. Maria Perez matter-of-factly describes the medical care and subsequent death of her first child: "She died when she was one year old. She had ear infections and then a high fever and went into the hospital one day and died the next. Three or four days before I brought her to the doctor and told him that she wasn't well and that she wasn't eating and he said, 'Oh, that's all right. Just give her rice and beans.' He gave her some injections and sent us home. Maybe he could have done something for her then."

Would the same doctor have told the wife of a lawyer from the suburbs or the wife of a corporate executive from the Upper East Side of New York "just give her rice and beans" and then have sent them home? Or is this story just one example of the class bias of physicians who are almost invariably white, from middle- or upper-middle-class backgrounds and, until recently, overwhelmingly male, but who are providing care for poor or working class members of minority groups?[15]

But Maria is not finished with her tale about medical care. She goes to see a psychiatrist because of her concern about the emotional development of her youngest child, and the psychiatrist, threatening a breach of confidentiality, gives her an ultimatum—she must tell the day care center that she is living with her husband and not separated from him as she has claimed in order to avoid paying for the day care, or the psychiatrist will tell the center. Again, would that psychiatrist have reacted in the same fashion to an instance of income tax evasion or a false insurance claim for a "bad back" by a woman of another class?

Elinor's experience is perhaps the most harrowing: "In all the time Michael was sick, only one thing really hurt my feelings. There's one doctor; she was a female doctor ... she made me feel so small ... she asked me, 'Is Michael your husband's child?' " This white physician is questioning the wife of a black postal clerk whose child is dying from sickle cell anemia. Since the doctor was female, simply recruiting more women into medicine is clearly not in itself the answer to the problem of humanizing the medical profession. Would this physician have asked these questions of a white, upper-middle-class mother whose dying child's diagnosis did not quite seem to concur with the facts? I think not. But these women survive the insults and the poor medical care; they have no other choice.

It became clear toward the end of my interviewing that the women were not focusing on women's health issues; in an attempt to elicit views about or experiences of birth control, abortion, and childbearing, I telephoned a few of them and asked about this specific area. Their responses were related almost entirely to the cutbacks in services of the municipal hospital system, the problems of obtaining medical care for those who cannot afford to pay, and the depersonalization and dehumanization of hospital-based medical care. Gwen, for example, told about being refused out-patient care because she had not been able to pay her bill, and said, "People don't go until they are really, really sick." She thinks that people are also intimidated by the arrogance of doctors and consequently do not play the role they should in their own well-being. On the specific subject of women's health, she prefers female doctors or at least female counselors because they are "more understanding" than male physicians.

Christina described the impersonal care she received when she gave birth to her daughter: "You're taken care of by interns—I'm not knocking internship—but you're treated like a machine. I got angry and didn't let anybody touch me. I refused to be examined because I was going through excess pain and I felt like a guinea pig."

She felt that the hospital treated childbirth as though it were like "having a tooth out or taking a splinter out. All they worry about is their schedule." Finally, she said that medical care is even more difficult to obtain now since New York City municipal hospitals have been cut back financially; now "it costs twenty-five dollars just to go to the emergency room."

Marion sums it up when she, no radical, says it is time for a national health service "just like in England" because medical care has become inaccessible—"At one time your doctor made a house call. Now if you call him for an emergency he makes an appointment ... You could be dying now, but the appointment has to be made for next week"—and because it has become too expensive. Furthermore, she has joined the thousands of Americans who have formed their own groups in order to deal with their medical and quasi-medical problems. The astonishing popularity of self-help groups is, I believe, in direct proportion to the dissatisfaction with the professional medical-care system, and, while there appear to be significant drawbacks to the increase in the number and variety of self-help groups in this country, these groups are often far more effective in dealing with a variety of health-related problems than are medical-care professionals.[16]

Education is yet another human service that these women criticize. Elinor is concerned about her son's failure in school. She connects his problem to the death of her younger son, but perhaps another educational system could have helped him to continue learning even in the face of such a trauma. Frances, an educational paraprofessional, describes the annual reduction in funds for special help for children with learning disabilities, and the chaos and uncertainty created by these cutbacks. She has attempted to persuade her son to obtain special training as a mechanic, but he resists her urging, and who can be sure which of them is right? According to Ivar Berg, in his study subtitled "The Great Training Robbery," little correlation exists between increased job training and job satisfaction, particularly among relatively "low-education, low-skilled" workers,[17] and frequently little correlation exists, particularly in blue-collar work, between additional education and job advancement.[18] Gwen is, of course, a clear example of how training can lead, not to jobs, but only to higher expectations and then to greater dissatisfaction when these expectations are not fulfilled.

Christina Ramos who has spent considerable time attempting to analyze the educational system describes the irrelevance of her own education and the deep-seated biases within the system: "I wasn't very good in English and I moved to Brooklyn at that time and they gave me some essay to do on Shakespeare. I didn't even know how to read that well and they told me to read Shakespeare. I wanted to see things being built, things being done, things that you could see, that you could touch and they gave me Shakespeare..."

She talks about the frustration that she felt in high school: "I don't know why I didn't learn in school; I wanted to learn. In school you have to go there and sit down and I'm not a person to be sitting down for all those tremendous hours. I needed to chat, to talk to people, to move around and to do ... The only time that I felt comfortable is when they put me in the nurse's office and I learned about filing. There I was given something concrete to do ... You could master it and feel good about it."

Then she goes on to delineate the particular educational barriers for black and Hispanic children—the teachers in her neighborhood school are predominantly white and middle class, and the children are predominantly black, Hispanic and poor. As a school aide she attempted to build up Black Studies Week but the teachers really didn't care. Basically she found that the institution didn't care about the children—it only cared about itself. It was only when she went to Hostos Community College, which is run by Spanish-Americans for Spanish-Americans, that she could make any sense of the educational process. There people were warm and friendly to her. There she saw men and women of her own ethnic background who had "made it" but were still humane and acted as though she was a human being. Christina is struggling to finish her education in spite of being a single parent, in spite of being unemployed, in spite of losing her job as a school aide because it was no longer funded. Although she speaks English fluently, if often metaphorically, she was recently refused a job in a bilingual program because "her English was not good enough."

The problems in our educational system begin even before primary school. The incredible inadequacy of American day care is poignantly illustrated by Maria Perez who is only one of millions of working women who are trying to make arrangements for the care of their preschool children without adequate community-supported day care resources. It has been estimated that one out of every three mothers with preschool children is holding down a job while there is room for only 900 thousand of their six million children—fifteen percent—in licensed child-care centers, many of which provide no more than custodial care.[19] Many centers are "part-day" and even those that are "full-day" are not open long enough to meet the needs of women who must go to work early in the morning and who work late at night or on weekends.[20]

Thus, the vast majority of working women must rely on traditional forms of child care such as baby sitters, relatives, or friends at a time when these forms of child care are becoming increasingly scarce in our fragmented, mobile society. Moreover, at a time when nearly two-thirds of American women think that the government should assist in providing child care on an "ability-to-pay basis" for those who need it,[21] the federal government is currently spending only approximately $1 billion a year on child care.[22] This may be compared to the $150 billion spent annually by the entire society on health care and medical care, the $22 billion spent on alcoholic beverages in a single year, the $14 billion spent for tobacco products and smokers' accessories in a single year, and the 675 billion less-deflated dollars of the 1960s spent on the war in Indochina.

Other industrialized societies—the Soviet Union, the Scandinavian countries, and Israel, for example[23]—have made a far larger commitment to child care than has the United States. Sweden, a country that matches or exceeds the United States in gross national product per person, in urbanization, and in level of technology, has provided care both in centers and in closely supervised "family day care" settings for sixty percent of all its preschool children who need day care because their parents are gainfully employed or studying, and it plans to provide care for eighty percent of those children by 1980.[24] Even developing countries such as China and Cuba have made a considerable commitment toward the care and well-being of children.[25] Our society's treatment of our children has led one observer to ask, "Do Americans *really* like children?" His answer is yes and no—an accurate description of our ambivalence toward children and toward our responsibility as a society for their well-being.[26]

Our society is ambivalent not only toward children but also toward working mothers. Each of the countries mentioned above has not only made a commitment to the collective care of children but also has accepted, to a considerable degree, the desirability of women working outside of the home, and, in some cases, has actively called upon women to enter the labor force. With the official unemployment rate in the United States hovering around seven percent there is little direct or indirect encouragement for women to work; the lack of child care facilities may in part be viewed as a social policy intended to discourage women from entering the labor force.

What is the result of this policy on the individual woman? The woman of modest income, income above the welfare level but below a comfortable, affluent level, frequently has extraordinary difficulty obtaining adequate child care for a price she can pay. Moreover, she is encouraged by the structure of human service institutions to lie, as Maria Perez has said, in order to "make a decent life." Or as Gwen Johnson has commented, "There's a whole lot of ins and outs because of the way the society is set up. They set you up to make you untruthful . . . to make you dishonest." Can a society as wealthy as ours afford to drive its citizens to the conflict, the guilt, and the humiliation that Maria has suffered in order to provide adequately for her family?

A recent example of legislation that forces the poor to lie in order to gain equitable access to services is the law that forbids payment for an abortion under Medicaid unless it is necessary to save the woman's life or the pregnancy results from incest or rape. The reported incidence of incest and rape is likely to increase markedly as poor women find that that is their only path to obtaining abortions that more affluent women can simply purchase without problem or stigma.

Hardship and struggle are not new experiences to many of these women; most of them knew considerable poverty as children. In fact all except Diane, whose father supported his family in style through extralegal methods, and Maria, whose family was relatively comfortable economically in Ecuador but whose economic situation deteriorated sharply when she came to this country, knew poverty as children. Rose's family farm in Ireland yielded barely enough food to feed their large family; her father was forced to go to England for a long period of time to find work. Marion's mother was on home relief, and Marion vividly describes the shame and humiliation she felt at having to stand in line for handouts; she vows she will never do it again. Elinor's mother was also on welfare; Gwen grew up on 100th Street amidst the junkies.

Christina vividly describes her family's economic situation: Her mother was "just trying to make it day to day with five children . . . like in the school . . . they tell you that you have to wear a gym suit and you have to wear sneakers and you have to do this and you have to do that, (but) that takes money. Or they have to take you to the doctor . . . that takes money. Maybe they couldn't do it because they didn't have the money." Not only was her family unable to provide the basics, but Christina points out that society paints a picture of affluence and success but does not help the individual reach that remote and unattainable level of ease and comfort: "Even on television . . . so and so was a doctor and so and so was a PTA president. The kids grew up and they're going to college . . . How do they do it? They don't tell you how to get there. They assume, then you assume . . . but how *do* they get there? And where did they get the money? And how come they have money and we don't have money?" And then perhaps the ultimate indictment: ". . . the city doesn't supply anything. It doesn't supply you with a fruit, with a banana, it doesn't even supply you with a mango . . ."

These women started with next to nothing. They had only their own initiative, perseverance, and willingness to struggle; the fact that they are living relatively comfortable lives today is due, for the most part, to their own efforts. Marion DeLuca remembers: " . . . when we got married we didn't have anything. We couldn't even afford to make our own wedding. All we had was twenty fingers between us. We really had to work for whatever we have. And whatever we have—our home, our car, our savings—whatever we have, he and I did together."

Perhaps not surprisingly, because most of these women struggled out of poverty themselves, many have somewhat negative feelings toward people who are now receiving welfare. Maria Perez says: "I think it's a terrible thing when people go on welfare. I never wanted to go on welfare even though they told me . . . that I could. I feel and my husband feels that if you have your two good hands to work with you should work. Maybe it's that I have too much pride." While Marion DeLuca feels that receiving public assistance during the 1930s was unavoidable, she thinks that these days many people choose not to work but rather to receive public assistance: "During the Depression my mother was on home relief and when we had to stand in line and wait for the clothes they would give us or the measly food they were handing out, it was miserable . . . that's why I can't see somebody standing around on a corner and I have to pay for it. We were there out of circumstances . . . not out of choice. But today a lot of these welfare cases are out of choice . . . and how many are stealing from the welfare out of choice? Yes, I do resent them."

On the other hand Marion thinks that those who are unable to care for themselves should be helped: "Nobody in our country should go hungry, nobody. We have elderly that need help, that's beautiful. We have young people that need help, fine . . ."

Marion further feels that any job is preferable to receiving welfare, but her view presumes that there are jobs to be found if the unemployed simply look for them. While there may indeed be a cultural gap between those who think, as Marion does, that no job is as demeaning as receiving welfare and those who think that people are more exploited by dead-end jobs that pay little or nothing more than public assistance,[27] there is ample evidence that the scarcity of jobs is only too real and that the true unemployment rate is far higher than the seven percent figure generally cited. Two groups are traditionally omitted from unemployment statistics: workers on involuntary part-time schedules and "workers who have become so despairing at their inability to find or keep jobs that they give up the search."[28] If we include these two groups, the national unemployment rate for 1976 becomes 10.1 percent rather than 7.7 percent.[29]

While Marion's point of view is understandable in the light of her own history, it becomes yet another form of "blaming the victim," an analysis that is encouraged by our social system and one that helps to divide the working class further from the poor. Job scarcity forces the working class and the poor to compete for the same jobs; those who are left unemployed are then blamed for not wanting to work. The working class is further victimized by an economic structure in which wages have not kept pace with inflation in recent years[30] and in which job insecurity, particularly in the service occupations, is a constant concern.

Another critical element in determining these working-class women's attitudes toward the poor and the near-poor is the issue of their personal safety. Several women expressed concern about this problem in their neighborhoods, not only in the evenings but during the day as well. Elinor Thomas who lives in a very well kept city housing project in a quiet, attractive neighborhood says she is cautious and somewhat fearful every time she gets into the elevator in her building and that she is reluctant to go out to meetings in the evening without her son or her husband. Marion DeLuca and her neighbors have formed a block association that has organized a civilian patrol to attempt to diminish crime in their neighborhood. Her descriptions of women being mugged in her neighborhood during the day, her unwillingness to take a subway except at rush hour or to drive to an evening meeting alone because she does not want to walk from the garage to her apartment alone, make it clear that her concerns about safety have altered her daily life. Rose O'Rourke was mugged at noontime while entering her apartment, and although she says she has gotten over the intense period of fear, she is, nonetheless, extremely careful now.

These women represent a large segment of the working class who, because they do not have the economic resources to move at will into safer neighborhoods, must continue to live on the fringe of poor areas while contiguous sections of their own neighborhoods become poorer and more dangerous each year. Except for Marion who is active in her block association, most of the women feel relatively helpless either to protect themselves or to reverse the ever-increasing crime rate. It is worth noting that Marion, the only woman who has turned to collective action, is also an active member of other mutual aid groups—her tenants' association and a self-help medical group.

Unfortunately, several of these women associate the reality of increasing crime with race, and their fear feeds on the separation, the gulf that exists among different groups in our society. Diane remembers when she first learned that Tony was Spanish: "It was two weeks after I was seeing him that I found out that he was Spanish, 'cause he never told me and he looked Italian...I asked him that day and he just laughed. But by then I didn't care." Gwen remembers her neighborhood when she was a child: "The Italians would harass the Puerto Ricans...Even blacks couldn't go past First Avenue 'cause the Italians owned First Ave...As I see it now, it was just a real fight for territory...You know when you're poor you're very narrowed into your community and you don't know too much about other people's community and when you go there you feel uncomfortable. So rather than put your self through all those changes you stay with what you know."

Christina describes the problem for members of minority groups in adjusting to a dominant Anglo-Saxon culture when they live in isolation from that culture: "Some of them (teachers) really believe that we are in America and because we are in America and they speak English, we should all be Anglo-Saxon. But we don't really ever see Anglo-Saxons...if you look at the communities throughout this city you have the Chinese section, you have the Jewish section, you have the Irish section, you have the Italian section, you have the Puerto Rican section, you have the black section. So everything around those kids, what they see, what they touch, all their senses tell them that they do not live in an Anglo-Saxon world."

What are the effects of this gulf that people feel? Diane describes her fear when she visited Tony's apartment in Harlem for the first time:

"And then he took me by his neighborhood . . . and I was so petrified. He says, 'I'm just going to check the mailbox.' I says, 'No. No. No, you're not leaving me in this car . . .' So he says, 'All right, I'll get one of my friends to stay with you.' He calls this Spanish guy with a big Afro. I was so scared." Thus, the combination of fear for one's own safety, fear of strangers, and the fact that blacks and Puerto Ricans earn significantly less than other members of the society and therefore live in large numbers in poorer neighborhoods on the fringe of working-class neighborhoods results in objective conditions that pit group against group. In addition, as Frances has pointed out, members of these groups are often in competition for the same scarce jobs.

It is not surprising that fear and suspicion, personal danger, and a job shortage separate these groups and cause hostility; what is surprising is that in spite of the problems with which these people must grapple from day to day they can still differentiate between a group toward which they may feel considerable hostility and individuals within that group whom they have come to know personally and to care for. Rose, for example, describes conditions in a number of apartment buildings in her neighborhood: "There is a large development near here which is pretty well shot. They're mugging them left and right there. But there's an awful lot of people moving out . . . anyone at all that can afford it . . . Puerto Ricans and blacks are moving in. Mostly black." Then she goes on to talk about a neighbor in her apartment building: "Now the nurse across the hall from me, she's black and I couldn't ask for a nicer person." Rose differentiates this nurse from other blacks in part because of her class background: "Of course, she's from a very good culture, she has two brothers, both doctors, and a brother an engineer, and her sister is the principal of a high school so she has a very good background." But later she individualizes on the basis of personal characteristics when she describes a "lovely" Puerto Rican family who were "working people, they were hard working people."

Marion admits honestly that she discriminates in her role as a member of the tenants' association, but while she clearly has very angry feelings toward many blacks and Hispanics she also singles out individuals and families for whom she has warm, positive feelings. It is important to note that she started out as a "Roosevelt Democrat" and has retained many traditionally liberal positions throughout the years. It seems as though Marion, who is representative of many members of the working class, has been driven to her current attitudes by a society that perpetuates competition for jobs, housing and scarce human services and in so doing divides rather than unites the poor and the working class and the various ethnic, racial, and religious groups within American society.

Finally, what have we learned about these eight women?

We know that they are hard working, resilient, flexible, yet tenacious; that some of them, particularly the younger women, are searching—for work, for education, for ways to balance their multiple responsibilities; that they live in a largely inhospitable environment in which their physical safety is a constant source of concern, in which adequate day care is an extremely scarce resource, in which the educational system often does not educate, in which the health care system is often insensitive, sometimes cruel and not infrequently discriminatory. We know that these women are separated from one another by fear—fear of the unfamiliar, fear of economic insecurity, fear of the poverty many of them have known all too well.

We also know that they are warm, caring human beings who reach out with love to their families and friends, recognizing that their lives are inextricably intertwined with the lives of those closest to them. They see themselves primarily as part of their family grouping, which often includes their parents, less frequently their brothers and sisters, and in one instance included a nephew. And while they recognize that their own needs are important, they state clearly that their struggle for survival includes attempting to meet the needs of all family members, even though that commitment frequently means compromising their own immediate wishes and goals. In a society that offers so few supports to the family, particularly to poor and working-class families, compromise and mutual caring become essential ingredients for survival.

These women recognize only too well that as individuals they are, to a large extent, powerless. Their consciousness of this powerlessness and of their economic position in American society has caused them to be wary of those aspects of the women's movement that emphasize individualism and personal fulfillment. Rather than falling prey to the narcissism, our form of the "cult of the individual," which characterizes so much of American society, these women have retained a sense of solidarity with their immediate families, with their extended families, with other members of the working class, or with their ethnic or racial group, and therefore they relate almost exclusively to those feminist issues which are economic in nature, such as equal pay and equal job opportunities. When I raised the issue of the role of women or the women's movement many of the women reacted as though those were distant concerns which had little or no immediate relevance to them. In general, they do not see themselves oppressed as women; if they, in fact, see themselves as oppressed at all, it is in the form of economic or racial oppression.

In earlier periods of American history women played a leading role in struggles against oppression. Perhaps one of the most dramatic and moving instances of women's participation in collective action was the 1912 strike of the Lawrence textile workers. By 1910 the town of Lawrence, Massachusetts, had a population of 86,000 of whom 35,000 were mill-workers. One-half of the children of Lawrence worked in textile mills where the hours were long, the pace of work fast, and the accident rate high. According to one source:

> Fingers and hands were easily crushed. Women and girls were sometimes scalped when their hair caught in the unguarded machinery . . . The extent of poverty and near starvation was appalling. Families depended on their wages to such an extent that pregnant women worked until just before their babies arrived, and some gave birth right in the mill between the looms.[31]

Organized by the IWW (Industrial Workers of the World) and spurred on by a pay cut, the workers walked out of the mills on January 11 and did not return to work for nine and one-half weeks, until their demands had been substantially met. During the strike a young female striker was killed, others were clubbed and beaten. In order to keep the workers' spirits high, parades were organized in which several thousand strikers marched around the city, accompanied sometimes by brass bands and always by singing. A verse they frequently sang was:

> As we come marching, marching, we bring the greater days.
> The rising of the women means the rising of the race.
> No more the drudge and idler—ten that toil where one reposes,
> But a sharing of life's glories: Bread and roses! Bread and roses! [32]

Women played such a key role in the Lawrence strike that strike leader William "Big Bill" Haywood has been quoted as saying, "The women won the strike." [33]

In recent years while few social and political organizations have been able to utilize effectively the strengths of these eight women and others like them—their commitment to the larger group, their view of themselves as part of a larger whole—there have been some relatively isolated instances of working-class women organizing and participating in collective action to improve the quality of their lives: the civil rights movement, particularly in the south, the efforts of office workers[34] and household workers[35] to unionize, anti-urban renewal groups, and perhaps the best-known current organization, the National Congress of Neighborhood Women.[36]

We must learn from these efforts and build on them, for if we are to create a more humane environment—one that will provide satisfying, secure jobs; adequate human services; safe neighborhoods in which residents can share a sense of community; and a more equitable distribution of wealth and power—ways must be found to form alliances across class lines and across racial and religious lines in order to organize collective action. The problems these eight women face are problems that are faced, to one degree or another, by all groups in our society. Perhaps their strengths, their strategies for survival, and their analyses of their world can help all of us to find ways of working together to build a more just and caring society.

Notes

INTRODUCTION

1. Barbara Mayer Wertheimer. *We Were There: The Story of Working Women in America.* New York: Pantheon Books, 1977, pp. 309–310.

2. Wertheimer, p. 310.

3. Wertheimer, pp. 294–295.

4. Wertheimer, p. 294.

5. Andrew Levison, *The Working-Class Majority.* New York: Penguin Books, 1974, p. 25.

6. Some of the recent books which have dealt with the issue of who is working class include Stanley Aronowitz, *False Promises: The Shaping of American Working Class Consciousness,* New York: McGraw-Hill, 1973; Harry Braverman, *Labor and Monopoly Capital: The Degradation of Work in the Twentieth Century,* New York: Monthly Review Press, 1974; Andrew Levison, *The Working-Class Majority,* New York: Penguin Books, 1974; Lillian Breslow Rubin, *Worlds of Pain: Life in the Working-Class Family,* New York: Basic Books, 1976.

7. Braverman, p. 359.

8. Aronowitz, pp. 11–12.

9. Braverman, p. 379.

10. Recent books on working-class women include Louise Kapp Howe, *Pink Collar Workers: Inside the World of Women's Work,* New York: Putnam, 1977; Joyce A. Ladner, *Tomorrow's Tomorrow: The Black Woman,* New York: Anchor Books, 1972; Gerda Lerner (Ed.), *Black Women in White America: A Documentary History,* New York: Vintage Books, 1973; Ann Oakley, *Woman's Work: The Housewife, Past and Present,* New York: Pantheon Books, 1974; Lillian Breslow Rubin, *Worlds of Pain: Life in the Working-Class Family,* New York: Basic Books, 1976; Nancy Seifer, *Nobody Speaks for Me! Self-Portraits of American Working Class Women,* New York: Simon & Schuster, 1976; Jean Tepperman, *Not Servants, Not Machines: Office Workers Speak Out,* Boston: Beacon Press, 1976; and Barbara Mayer Wertheimer, *We Were There: The Story of Working Women in America,* New York: Pantheon Books, 1977.

11. Braverman, p. 276.

12. Ivan Illich. *Medical Nemesis: The Expropriation of Health.* New York: Pantheon Books, 1976.

13. Bureau of Labor Statistics, *U.S. Department of Labor News* (Middle Atlantic Region, News Release), June 30, 1977, pp. 1–9.

REFLECTIONS

1. Barbara Everitt Bryant. *American Women Today and Tomorrow.* National Commission on the Observance of International Women's Year, Washington, D.C.: U.S. Government Printing Office, March 1977, p. 12.

2. Louise Kapp Howe. *Pink Collar Workers: Inside the World of Women's Work.* New York: Putnam, 1977, p. 21.

3. *The New York Times,* November 20, 1977.

4. *Consumer Income: Household Money Income in 1976 and Selected Social and Economic Characteristics of Households.* U.S. Government Printing Office, U.S. Department of Commerce, Bureau of the Census, Series P–60, No. 109, January 1978, p. 2.

5. Eli Zaretsky. *Capitalism, the Family, and Personal Life.* New York: Harper & Row, 1976, p. 17.

6. Frances Fox Piven and Richard A. Cloward. *Regulating the Poor: The Functions of Public Welfare.* New York: Vintage Books, 1972, p. 3.

7. Piven and Cloward, p. 261.

8. U.S. Bureau of Labor Statistics. Quoted in Paul Delancy, "Middle-Class Gains Create Tension in Black Community," in *The New York Times,* February 28, 1978.

9. David Vidal. "Dream Still Eludes Mainland Puerto Ricans," in *The New York Times,* September 11, 1977.

10. *Consumer Income: Household Money Income in 1976 and Selected Social and Economic Characteristics of Households.* U.S. Department of Commerce, Bureau of the Census, Series P–60, No. 109, January 1978, pp. 2–3.

11. Philip Shabecoff. "Why Blacks Still Don't Have Jobs," in *The New York Times,* September 11, 1977.

12. William Julius Wilson. "Poor Blacks' Future," in *The New York Times,* February 28, 1978.

13. Vidal.

14. For an excellent discussion of medicalization and social control, see Irving K. Zola. "Medicine as an Institution of Social Control," in Caroline Cox and Adrianne Med (Eds.). *A Sociology of Medical Practice.* London: Collier-Macmillan, 1975, pp. 170–185.

15. For a description of the race and social class background of health workers, see Vicente Navarro. *Medicine Under Capitalism.* New York: Prodist, 1976, pp. 135–145.

16. For an excellent, comprehensive discussion of the self-help movement, see Alan Gartner and Frank Riessman. *Self-help in the Human Services.* San Francisco: Jossey-Bass, 1977. For a discussion of some of the problems of self-help groups, see Victor W. Sidel and Ruth Sidel. "Beyond Coping," in *Social Policy.* September–October 1976, pp. 67–69.

17. Ivar Berg. *Education and Jobs: The Great Training Robbery.* Boston: Beacon Press, 1971, pp. 132–135.

18. Berg, pp. 89–90.

19. "Child Care Aid Is Held Lacking," in *The New York Times*, January 13, 1976.

20. Pamela Roby (Ed.). *Child Care–Who Cares?* New York: Basic Books, 1973, p. 6.

21. Bryant, p. 3.

22. "Child Care Aid Is Held Lacking," in *The New York Times*, January 13, 1976.

23. See, for example, Kitty Weaver, *Lenin's Grandchildren: Preschool Education in the Soviet Union*, New York: Simon & Schuster, 1971; Urie Bronfenbrenner, *Two Worlds of Childhood: U.S. and U.S.S.R.*, New York: Russell Sage Foundation, 1970; Melford E. Spiro, *Children of the Kibbutz: A Study in Child Training and Personality*, New York: Schocken, 1965; and Bruno Bettelheim, *Children of the Dream*, New York: Avon, 1971.

24. Siv Thorsell. "Pre-school Education and Child Care in Sweden," in *Current Sweden* (No. 155), March 1977, pp. 1–9.

25. See Ruth Sidel, *Women and Child Care in China: A Firsthand Report*, New York: Penguin Books, 1973; William Kessen (Ed.), *Childhood in China*, New Haven: Yale University Press, 1975; Marvin Leiner, *Children Are the Revolution: Day Care in Cuba*, New York: Viking Press, 1974; and Karen Wald, *Children of Che: Child Care and Education in Cuba*, Palo Alto, Calif.: Ramparts Press, 1978.

26. Kenneth Keniston, "Children as Victims: The Emptying Family," in *The New York Times*, February 18, 1976.

27. Susan H. Gray and Louis Bolce. "Not That Job, Thanks," in *The New York Times*, December 5, 1977.

28. Richard B. Duboff. "Unemployment in the United States: An Historical Summary," in *Monthly Review*, November 1977, pp. 10–24.

29. Duboff.

30. Peter Khiss. "New York City's Factory Wages Went Up by 80%, but Bought Less," in *The New York Times*, May 15, 1977.

31. Wertheimer, pp. 355–358.

32. Wertheimer, p. 366.

33. Wertheimer, p. 353.

34. Tepperman.

35. Seifer, pp. 138–177.

36. Carol Brightman. "The Women of Williamsburg," in *Working Papers for a New Society*. January/February 1978, pp. 50–57. Constance Rosenblum. "Family and Feminism in Williamsburg," in *Sunday News Magazine*, August 7, 1977, pp. 12–14, 29.

Bibliography

Arnow, Harriette. *The Dollmaker.* New York: Avon, 1972.

Arnowitz, Stanley. *False Promises: The Shaping of American Working Class Consciousness.* New York: McGraw-Hill, 1973.

Autobiography of Mother Jones, The. Chicago: Charles H. Kerr, 1976.

Braverman, Harry. *Labor and Monopoly Capital: The Degradation of Work in the Twentieth Century.* New York: Monthly Review Press, 1974.

Foner, Philip S. (Ed.). *The Factory Girls.* Urbana, Illinois: University of Illinois Press, 1977.

Gans, Herbert J. *The Urban Villagers.* New York: Free Press, 1965.

Howe, Louise Kapp. *Pink Collar Workers: Inside the World of Women's Work.* New York: Putnam, 1977.

Howell, Joseph T. *Hard Living on Clay Street: Portraits of Blue Collar Families.* New York: Anchor Books, 1973.

Kahn, Kathy. *Hillbilly Women: Mountain Women Speak of Struggle and Joy in Southern Appalachia.* New York: Avon, 1974.

Ladner, Joyce A. *Tomorrow's Tomorrow: The Black Woman.* New York: Anchor Books, 1972.

Lerner, Gerda (Ed.). *Black Women in White America: A Documentary History.* New York: Vintage Books, 1973.

Levison, Andrew. *The Working-Class Majority.* New York: Penguin Books, 1974.

Mitchell, Juliet. *Woman's Estate.* New York: Pantheon Books, 1971.

Oakley, Ann. *Woman's Work: The Housewife, Past and Present.* New York: Pantheon Books, 1974.

Olsen, Tillie. *Yonnondio.* New York: Delacorte Press, 1974.

Reiter, Rayna R. (Ed.). *Toward an Anthropology of Women.* New York: Monthly Review Press, 1975.

Rosaldo, Michelle Zimbalist, and Lamphere, Louise (Eds.). *Woman, Culture and Society.* Stanford, California: Stanford University Press, 1974.

Rosen, Ruth, and Davidson, Sue (Eds.). *The Maimie Papers.* Old Westbury, N.Y.: The Feminist Press, 1977.

Rubin, Lillian Breslow. *Worlds of Pain: Life in the Working-Class Family.* New York: Basic Books, 1976.

Ryan, William. *Blaming the Victim.* New York: Vintage Books, 1972.

Seifer, Nancy. *Nobody Speaks for Me! Self-Portraits of American Working Class Women.* New York: Simon & Schuster, 1976.

Sennett, Richard, and Cobb, Jonathan. *The Hidden Injuries of Class.* New York: Knopf, 1973.

Tepperman, Jean. *Not Servants, Not Machines: Office Workers Speak Out!* Boston: Beacon Press, 1976.

Wertheimer, Barbara Mayer. *We Were There: The Story of Working Women in America.* New York: Pantheon Books, 1977.

Zaretsky, Eli. *Capitalism, the Family and Personal Life.* New York: Harper & Row, 1976.